Your Voice in Demand

The AuthorHouse Guide to Marketing and Promoting Your Book

authorHOUSE™

1663 LIBERTY DRIVE, SUITE 200
BLOOMINGTON, INDIANA 47403
(800) 839-8640
WWW.AUTHORHOUSE.COM

First published by AuthorHouse 09/19/05

ISBN: 1-4208-8008-X (e)
ISBN: 1-4208-7897-2 (sc)

Printed in the United States of America
Bloomington, Indiana

This book is printed on acid-free paper.

Contents

Introduction

Promoting Your Book

You don't have to be a marketing expert to create, manage, and execute an effective marketing campaign for your book. Now that you are a published author, you have the opportunity to tell the world about your book, share your creation, and drive sales. How you approach this aspect of publishing depends on your goals, resources, skills, and the amount of effort you are willing to expend. However you decide to approach this exciting aspect of being a published author, the more of "you" that you put into the process, the better your chances for success.

As you begin the process of marketing and selling your book, you should keep in mind that your book will be competing in a crowded marketplace. According to Bowker, the publishing industry in the United States produced over 195,000 titles in 2004. Don't, however, let this statistic discourage you! Instead, use this knowledge as you develop goals for marketing your own book, and realize that to carve out your book's success within this exciting arena, you need a well-thought-out marketing plan.

Understanding the implications of leveraging print-on-demand for fulfillment will also have a bearing on how you market your book. Print-on-demand technology is still relatively new in the world of book publishing. As occurs with any revolutionary change in a time-honored industry, understanding and acceptance of the technology has not evolved as rapidly as the technology itself. Many traditional publishers and booksellers maintain the perception that self-published books are inherently not as good as those from traditional publishing houses. With your own published book in hand, you have solid proof that this is absolutely not the case.

You, and others like you, are breaking down these barriers and proving that self-published books meet or exceed the quality of traditionally published books. Self-publishing and print-on-demand technology are rapidly gaining in recognition and popularity. By making it possible to print books as they're needed, rather than warehousing costly stockpiles of copies well in advance of their actual sale date, the fulfillment process can be more responsive to customer demand. In addition, print-on-demand has enabled the publication of a wide range of information that might never have found a "voice" without this innovative technology.

Just as no one else could tell your story or share information the way you have, no one else is as uniquely suited to promote the compelling value of that work. You are the most important element of your book's marketing program. No one will care more about maximizing your book's sales than will you. As the creator and driving force behind your book's marketing and promotion campaign, you can concentrate your marketing time and energies on your book alone. You aren't trying to sell a "line" of books or a long list of miscellaneous titles from a publisher's annual publishing plan. When you market your book, you're selling nothing but you and your voice; this dedicated focus is your best tool in finding a strong niche for your book in the marketplace. What happens is up to you.

Chapter 1

Creating a Marketing and Promotion Plan

You've worked hard to produce your book, and the next step is to start working on your book's marketing plan. It is never too early to begin formulating your marketing plan, as many of your marketing efforts will require time to produce results. If your book isn't finished yet, you may even be able to launch parts of your marketing campaign in the months preceding your book's actual publication date. The sooner you can get started, the sooner you can have an impact on your book's sales.

Deciding how to best market and promote your book involves careful planning. No one can control the marketplace, however, and even the most careful planning won't guarantee specific results. But you can't hope to maximize your book's sales through random acts of salesmanship. A carefully structured and detailed plan is your best "boost" toward getting the most sales and the widest distribution of your work.

Determining Your Target Audience

To create a marketing plan that will achieve the best results for the least amount of investment, you must know precisely *who* your book will appeal to. With that information in mind, you'll be able to craft a marketing plan that is best able to reach those readers.

Most books appeal to multiple types of readers, but your early marketing efforts should be directed toward the individuals and groups who will be *most* interested in your book. If your marketing plan is too broad in its early stages, it can lose its focus and become ineffective. By setting up your marketing plan for early success, you can feed even greater success down the road.

Pinpoint Your Book's Benefits

Begin by developing a clear and concise statement of exactly what your book offers readers. Consider the book's content, purpose, and message:

~ When a reader finishes your book, what new knowledge, understanding, or skill set will he or she have gained from the experience?

~ Does your book show people how to create something? Does it outline the steps for accomplishing a task?

~ Does your book offer insights or unique perspectives into common life stages, issues, or problems?

~ Does your book fall into a subset of a popular genre? For example, is it a historical mystery or forensic suspense novel?

~ Can readers save time or money using the information you provide?

~ Does your book offer information useful for people who have no previous experience in your book's topic area, or are its benefits greater for intermediate and advanced audiences?

~ Is your book solely for entertainment, offering readers an opportunity to relax over an engaging story?

~ What makes your book unique? Among all of the books published on your topic, what does your book offer that most others don't?

~ Does your book address issues, ideas, or interests that would appeal to a specific community, region, or other locale?

~ Is your book like others that have been successful, such that you can use their success to help you define, reach, and market to target groups?

When you've considered all of these points, write one or two sentences that describe your book's content or message and the specific need or desire it fulfills for readers.

If you have trouble pinpointing your book's benefit this specifically, step back and consider your own experience. If you understand why you wrote your book and what you learned in the process, you may gain a clearer understanding of the unique benefit others will gain from reading your work.

Researching Your Target Audience

With a clear and simple statement of your book's benefits, you're ready to consider just which readers will be interested in those benefits. The first step is to do some basic research to define specifically what types of people will be included in your target audience. The library, bookstores, and the Internet offer numerous sources of information for finding your target audience.

Scan the magazine rack of your library or large bookstore for periodicals and journals related to the topic of your book, and use them to gather information about your potential book buyers. What types of social and professional organizations cater to the types of people who would benefit from your book's information? Who do the advertisements in related magazines and journals target? What are the backgrounds of the people who contributed articles to these publications? All of this information can help you gain a clearer picture of the types of readers you'll be targeting in your book.

Take time to browse through bookstores and online bookseller sites to learn about other available books in your genre or topic area, and how they're being pitched to potential buyers. Take a look at books on marketing and sales available in those bookselling sites. All of this research will help improve your marketing skills, and your understanding of the best techniques for marketing *your* book.

Internet searches can reveal a series of fast profiles of the types of issues, publications, organizations, and interests associated with your book's topic, to help you gather information about your target audience. Use any search engine, such as Google (*www.google.com*) or Yahoo! (*www.yahoo.com*), to scour the Web for information on your book's topic and readers. Go to the search engine site, type in the term or phrase you want to research, press Return or click the on-screen "Go" command, and the engine will return a number of results for your review.

Suppose, for example, that you've written a book on dog care and training. Using this example, you could turn up valuable information about your target audience by searching online under a number of terms, including "dog training groups," "dog care publications," "dog associations," and so on. If you've determined that your book offers a unique approach to housebreaking, search on "dog housebreaking." When your search results appear, visit the sites that seem most relevant, and try to determine the individuals and groups those sites are targeting with their messages. Most sites will offer advertising and links to other sites and vendors that can give you valuable information about the groups and individuals who are interested in your book's topic.

Although target audience research may seem daunting to you at first, some of your work has already been done for you. Various marketing organizations and publishers have developed a number of directories of groups, publications, organizations, and activities—information that you can use as you hone in on your target audience. Here are a few of the many online and print publications you can use to help identify the people who might be most interested in reading your book:

~ **Media directories:** Publications such as the *All in One Directory* by Gebbie Press (*www.gebbieinc.com*) and *Bacon's* (*www.bacons.com*) are great sources for listings of radio, television, and newspapers, as well as trade and consumer publications. SRDS (*www. srds.com*) also provides a directory of magazines by category that includes advertising rates and other data. Gale Research Directory, available in most libraries, also offers a media directory with extensive contact information.

~ **Encyclopedia of Associations:** Use this resource, published by the Gale Research Company and available in most libraries, to find information about professional, business, and trade associations, as well as chambers of commerce, charities, fan clubs, social and collegiate fraternities, and a wide range of local community organizations. This directory not only includes membership information, but it also lists trade show and convention information for these groups, as well as publications and newsletters that serve them.

~ **Directories of Periodicals:** A number of resources offer comprehensive lists of periodicals and journals. *Bacon's Magazine Directory* and the *Standard Periodical Directory* by Oxbridge Press are just two of these resources; check your library for others. Online, the *National Directory of Magazines* offers a list of publications that you can search by subject, title, author, and other criteria (*www.publist.com*).

And don't forget about your personal experience. Most likely, you are very familiar with your book's topic; how have you found information on this topic in the past? Where have you purchased books related to that topic, and what were your goals in purchasing those books? What organizations and activities do you participate in that put you in contact with others who are interested in your topic?

Prioritizing Your List

Next, use the information you've gathered to put together a list of all of the types of people that will fall into your target audience. Although you won't initiate your marketing campaign by targeting *everyone* on this list, it's important to make the list as all-inclusive as possible. Using the dog care and training example, the list might look like this:

~ Dog enthusiasts

~ New dog owners

~ Friends and family of dog owners

~ Dog trainers

~ Dog breeders

~ Veterinarian's assistants

~ Pet shop owners and employees

~ Kennel workers

~ Pet "house-sitters"

~ Dog groomers

~ Humane societies

~ Dog rescue groups

~ 4-H clubs

~ Dog training/kennel clubs

~ Manufacturers of dog training aids and toys

Now, because your first marketing efforts will target the individuals and groups on this list that are *most* likely to be interested in and benefit from your book, your next step is to rank the list. Use the description of your book's specific benefits to help determine which of the groups are most likely to be your book's buyers; rank those groups first on your list, and arrange others in descending order. As you create your marketing plan, the majority of your early-stage efforts will be aimed at the first part of your list. Throughout the course of your marketing program, you'll want to market to everyone on the list, of course—and the list may grow considerably as your experience and marketing contacts build. But when you're determining where to make your greatest initial investments in marketing time and dollars, work from the beginning of the list down.

Tracking the Locations of Your Target Audience

In the course of defining your target audience, you will have uncovered valuable information about where you can find the types of people within it. Understanding *where* to reach your target audience is critical to a successful marketing campaign. Again, draw upon your own experience as well as your research to identify the most likely venues for reaching people who would be interested in and benefit from reading your book. Where do members of your target audience live, work, shop, and gather? What online sites are frequently linked to or advertised on sites dealing with your book's topic? Where did *you* last learn about or purchase a book on this topic?

Important marketing locations will reach multiple groups within your target audience. For example, your book can reach many first-time dog owners at pet shops, veterinarians' offices, and humane societies—locations that also reach other members of your target audience. But don't stop at these "plum" locations; be innovative as you consider and research potential sites for marketing your book. You want to develop a wide variety of distribution channels for your book, including:

~ Book clubs

~ Professional/enthusiast associations

~ Bookstores and specialty retailers

~ Festivals, fundraisers, and other events

~ Online outlets

~ Businesses

~ Libraries and schools

Determining Your Marketing Goals and Sales Expectations

If you don't know where you want to go, you'll have a hard time getting there. This simple, logical statement should be a powerful guide to you as you craft your marketing plan. If you want to determine the best way to market your book, you first must know specifically what you want to accomplish with your marketing program.

Your goals in writing the book translate directly to your marketing goals. If you primarily are interested in seeing your story in print and distributing it to a small group of family and friends, you'll use a very different marketing approach than if you hope to reach a very wide audience. The more copies you hope to sell and the more widespread recognition you seek, the more time, energy—and money—you'll need to invest in your marketing efforts.

Aligning Hope and Reality

A good marketing plan is based on realistic expectations. Bear in mind the publishing statistics cited earlier as you frame your expectations of what may or may not be possible. For example, here are a few maxims held by many authors:

1. "I want to get my book on **Oprah** or **Larry King Live**." Nationally syndicated television shows receive hundreds if not thousands of requests every week, so national television coverage of your book is highly unlikely. Most major shows and television personalities won't accept unsolicited titles, press releases, or other marketing materials. A smart marketing campaign, therefore, won't sink much investment in trying to reach this venue.

2. "My book should be on bookstore shelves across the country." Most books enter national bookstore chains through book buyers, and they are very selective in what they choose to put on their stores' shelves. That's not to say that these chains are unreachable for you, however; through book signings and other local promotional efforts, you could gain placement for your book in a regional representative of a major bookstore chain. If you do well locally, you could catch the attention of the retailer and gain more widespread distribution.

3. "If I spend enough money on marketing, my book will be a success." While it is true that you will need to make a marketing investment to promote and sell your book, you need to make sure that you set realistic expectations and establish a budget that is right for you. The prudent tactic is to start with

realistic expectations and use your success to fund future efforts.

These facts aren't meant to discourage you, but to help you as you formulate reasonable goals for your book's sales. By focusing on the very real success you can achieve with your marketing campaign, you're better able to invest your time, energy, and dollars in efforts that can produce real rewards.

Start Locally, then Grow

None of this should discourage you from taking on challenging goals. Just be certain, however, that those goals are attainable. Begin your campaign by focusing your efforts on local promotions, then work your way out to larger regions and markets. Promoting your book locally will be more cost-effective and successful than tackling the difficulties of achieving nationwide distribution.

As you gain a greater understanding of your book's audience and marketplace, you can expand your marketing efforts. The more early success you can achieve, therefore, the better able you'll be to build toward even greater success through the course of your marketing campaign.

Outlining Your Marketing Budget

Finding distribution channels is important, but you'll need to promote your book in order to reach those channels. As you set your budget, you can determine how broad your promotional efforts can be, and what types of promotional activities are cost-effective for your plan *and* budget.

Say, for example, that you can allocate no more than $1,000 to your marketing budget. You'll need to handle almost all of the marketing activities on your own, and therefore will be investing a great deal of your time in the effort. You'll also need to rely on no-cost or low-cost promotional activities, including:

~ Word-of-mouth publicity

~ Making guest-speaker appearances at local organizations

~ Soliciting book reviews, interviews, and media appearances

~ Distributing press releases

~ Writing articles related to your book's topic, for publication in print media

~ Creating your own Web site to promote the book

~ Offering free copies of your book as door prizes, raffle prizes, or event giveaways

If your marketing goals are considerably larger, however, you'll probably need to invest more money in your budget. Distributing press kits with review copies, photographs, bookmarks and other marketing materials requires some investment, as do direct mail advertising and advertisement in local media outlets. Advertising in national markets, purchasing trade show booths, and a large online marketing campaign are among more costly promotional activities you can include in a heftier marketing budget. Setting up author tours or arranging for personal appearances at major events can require a significant investment of time and highly honed skills in self-promotion, in addition to the expenses of related travel.

Think carefully about the amount of time and money you can comfortably invest in your marketing plan, and then create a plan that fits well with your ability to invest.

Creating a Timeline for Your Marketing Plan

Now that you know who you're marketing to, where you need to do that marketing, and how much you'll spend on the program, you're ready to map out the timeline for your marketing plan. Although you're going to want to get your book's sales off to a strong start, you want to design a marketing campaign that will be effective for the long haul, not a short-lived blitz that won't bring you sustained sales.

Creating a Campaign for the "Long Haul"

The sales life of the average book is about three years, so your marketing campaign should extend over that same time period. Plan to hit the first year hard, making your most intense investments of time and money in that year's marketing activities. Then, you should devise a plan for each of the next two years that focuses on maintaining and building on your book's sales.

> Be sure to coordinate your marketing activities with your book's publishing schedule. Although some pre-publication marketing activities are important for developing sales, you'll kill sales opportunities if you don't have the product available for a waiting buyer. You don't want to schedule an author signing, for example, to take place before the book is available for purchase.

Some promotional activities can take place before your book is complete. You can begin writing press releases, preparing media materials (a book description, author bio, promotional bookmarks, and so on) in the weeks preceding your book's publication. Distributing press releases, scheduling author signings, soliciting book reviews, and carrying out direct sales campaigns are all events that work best immediately upon publication and in the first year after your book is published.

As you plan your marketing schedule, don't forget to plan for holidays, festivals, professional gatherings, and other organizational events that will offer prime selling opportunities for your book. Your target audience research will help you in determining when and where special sales opportunities exist, so you can hit the right markets at the right times. Is there a large annual golf tournament in your area that will offer sales opportunities for your golfing book? When should you plan to promote your book of college reminiscences in order to coordinate with sales opportunities at your university's homecoming festival? Are you targeting holiday gift-givers with your book? If so, plan to schedule promotional events well in advance, to maximize those sales.

In the remaining two years of your three-year plan, you can concentrate your sales efforts on maintaining sales. Web-based marketing offers, print advertising, scheduled speaking engagements, and expanded retail sales outlets are all promotional activities appropriate to years two and three of your marketing campaign.

Marketing as a Work in Progress

You may well need to return to and adjust your plan as you gain experience in your marketplace. As you learn about how your book is received by buyers, and gain more experience marketing to more buyer types, you'll develop new and more effective ways to identify and reach your audience.

If you come to the realization that sales have dried up and your plan is no longer working, go back through the process outlined in this chapter to rethink and revise your plan as necessary. Perhaps your target audience has shifted, audience needs have changed, or you've exhausted a once-viable market. Revisit and revise your plan as necessary, but by all means, remain committed to carrying it out.

Remember that promoting your book is an ongoing effort, not a short-term event. If you continue to develop and follow your marketing plan over a long period, you will sell more books—it's that simple. This type of sustained marketing program is especially essential if you are committed to reaching a broad audience with your work. Through careful planning and persistence, you can build upon a local word-of-mouth campaign to develop a far-reaching national marketing program that brings your book the recognition—and sales—it deserves.

Chapter 2

Web Marketing

The closest, easiest-to-use, and most effective marketplace available to you is on the Web. What's more, the Internet is the fastest-growing marketplace for books, and on-line book sales are poised to surpass sales through traditional retail outlets. As a published author, you're in a great position to take advantage of the Web as both a powerful marketing and sales tool. From purchasing a simple domain name to hosting your own Web log (most commonly known as a "blog"), you have a wide range of options for taking your book's sales to the Web. And don't worry that you're too far out of the technology loop to take advantage of Web markets; for a relatively minor investment of time and money, *anyone* can wage an effective Web marketing campaign.

Creating a Web Site

You don't need to be a Web site designer to have a professional-looking Web site that helps promote and sell your book. Cyberspace abounds with companies that can handle every phase of the process, including:

~   Designing and building your Web page

~   Hosting your Web site (everything from supplying a domain name to providing statistics on who visits, and when Web visitors are on your site)

~   Managing the site (responding to visitor interactions, updating information, and so on)

The amount of assistance you need depends upon how much involvement you choose to have with the process. To demonstrate the range of possibilities, here are just some of the options for these services:

~ You can hire a service to create a custom-designed Web site, host the site online, respond to visitor contacts, and update all information on a daily, weekly, or other schedule. Typically, these services charge for the initial design, in addition to monthly fees for hosting and managing the site.

~ You can choose a Web site design from templates available from a Web site design service. The service's tutorials walk you through the process of choosing a template and plugging in your information, uploading your photos, and so on. Typically, these services also host your site for a monthly fee. Again, most of these services offer tutorials to help you with updating your site and managing interactions with visitors.

~ You can use a Web design software package such as Moveable Type to create your own Web site, using or modifying the software's templates (learn more at *www.moveabletype.org*). You then can contract with a Web hosting service to host the site online. Starter Web hosting packages are relatively inexpensive and typically include a domain name, some basic Web design tools, and technical support services to help you launch your book's "Web presence."

~ At the most basic level, you can simply purchase a domain name, such as "yourbook.com" and let that name point to the AuthorHouse bookstore site. You will need to renew the name registration each year.

Choosing a URL and Domain Name for Your Site

Your first decision when creating a Web marketing site will be the choice of your site's domain name, which will appear in its Web address, or URL (uniform resource locator). A URL identifies the location of Web pages on the Internet. In the URL "http://www.yoursampledomainname.com", the domain name is "yoursampledomainname"; the letters preceding the domain name identify the protocol used to access the address, and the suffix ".com" is the most commonly used suffix for commercial sites. More than one domain name can point to the same Web site. Registering a domain name requires a fee, which may need to be paid yearly.

Of course, you can't choose a domain name that's already in use. A public domain name database, known as Whois, tracks domain names and can verify whether specific names are already registered; visit *www.whois.net* for more information.

Ideally, your domain name should reflect the way potential visitors will think of you and your book, making your URL relatively "intuitive" for the public. You need to choose carefully to make your URL address easy to learn and use. Here are some simple rules for choosing a good domain name and URL:

1. Choose a domain name and URL that are short, logical, and easy to remember. You might choose some form of your name (susansmith.com), for example, or the title of your book (darkwater.com). If your book title is long, considering shortening it; goodeats.com, for example, will be easier for visitors to remember than goodeatingfrommaineto california.com.

2. Try to avoid words that are difficult to spell or hard to remember. If your name is Michael Zabloskonowsky, for example, you may not want to use that name as a basis for the URL of a Web site marketing your first book, because many people will have difficulty remembering the spelling. MichaelZ.com, on the other hand, might work well. If your book title includes a word that's commonly misspelled (or is it "mispelled"?), you might want to register your domain name for multiple addresses. So, if your book is titled *The Proud Misspeller,* you might register the domain names proudmisspeller and proudmispeller to point to your Web site's URL, so that readers will find you under both spellings.

3. You might want to register multiple versions of your domain name with different suffixes, such as susansmith.com and susansmith.net, just to be sure that someone else with a too-similar domain name doesn't end up with visitors who were looking for your site.

4. Ask your friends, relatives, and co-workers what they think of a domain name you are considering. If they can't remember it or think that it doesn't seem logical for your site, try to come up with a better name.

No matter what kind of Web site you decide to host, be sure to drive people to it. Put your site address on your stationery and in your automatic "signature" on every e-mail message you send. Mention the address in speaking appearances, interviews, and press releases. The more traffic you drive to your site, the more potential sales it will generate.

Choosing Effective Content for Your Site

Remember that your Web site is designed to market your book. Therefore, you can include in it much of the same material that you make available in your media kits and other handouts. Here are just some of the types of information you might want to include in a basic Web site:

~ Information about your book, table of contents, and excerpts

~ Author biography

~ Press releases

~ List of upcoming book signings and speaking engagements

~ Upcoming events related to your book and its topic areas

~ Testimonial quotes, reviews of your book, published articles, and interviews by or about you

~ Link to the online sales portal for your book

~   Links to other sites related to your book's genre and
    topic (see the section "Setting Up Reciprocal Links"
    at the end of this chapter on how to get those sites to
    link back to you)

One thing to consider as you add information to your site
is that many Internet users still rely on dial-up connections
to access the Internet. Large files, such as graphic images,
will take a long time to load on the screens of these viewers.
Also consider that background music and sound effects can
annoy readers and cause an unpleasant disruption for those
in the area of your visitor's computer, so think carefully
before incorporating automatic sound effects into your site.
Follow the guidelines of your template instructions to make
your site fast and easy to use.

Managing Ongoing Fees

Your marketing Web site will require some financial
investment, but you can keep costs to a minimum by shopping
around and making careful choices in Web design, hosting,
and management.

You will need to plan on paying an annual fee for the
registration of your domain name. You can also plan on
paying a monthly fee for your Web hosting service. Most
Web design sites charge a one-time fee only. Some companies
provide multiple services—Web site templates, domain name
registration, e-mail, and hosting—for a single monthly fee.
To find companies offering any or all of these services, use
Google, Yahoo!, or any major search engine to search under
the appropriate terms ("domain name registration," "Web
hosting service," and "Web site design", for example).

If a site advertises any of these services at no charge or at an incredibly low charge, consider it a red flag and read the fine print. Every service has to earn money somehow, and a site that doesn't charge directly will charge in some other (potentially more costly) manner. The site might commandeer your e-mail list, for example, or otherwise take control of your site. Other lost-cost or free Web hosts will impose pop-up or banner ads that will appear when your Web site is visited. You want complete control over your Web site, so be willing to pay a reasonable fee to secure it.

Building and Maintaining a Blog

One of the most powerful online forms of communication to emerge has been the Web log, or "blog." The people who write and manage these sites—known as bloggers—use them to put their ideas, thoughts, views, and interests before the world. Carrying every type of information from simple Web "diaries" to highly charged political commentary, blogs have become increasingly common—and powerful.

Many journalists, professionals, and consumers regularly visit blogs to read opinions, follow current events, and uncover information on topics of shared interest. By offering news and links associated with your book, its topic, and genre, your blog can help you directly reach out to your book's target audience. As such, a blog can be an especially cost-effective marketing technique.

You can use your blog to market your book in a number of ways. Not only does your blog give you an opportunity to talk about your book and the events surrounding it, you also can use your blog commentary to build interest in your book's topic or genre, and to encourage reviews, gather reader quotes, correspond directly with your readers, and link visitors directly to your book's sales portal.

Running a blog is a great way to gather information about other published works competing with your book. In addition to encouraging and responding to letters and opinions from your blog readers, you also can review other publications that share your book's topic area or genre. Including book reviews on your site has multiple advantages for your own book's marketing campaign:

~ Your blog address will be returned as a result for any search conducted on the title of any book you've reviewed. If you review a book with strong public relations momentum, you can drive a large number of readers to your site.

~ You can arrange for a reciprocal review from the Web site or blog of the author of any book you review. When other sites review your book, you get even more publicity, and you increase your options for gathering great review quotes.

In order for your blog to be effective, however, you'll need to be sure that its information is accurate, reliable, current, and complete. Respond to letters and queries you receive on your blog, and be sure that you update it regularly. Also, be professional in stating your opinions. Although "rant" sites have gained great followings, be sure that your blog content and presentation are designed to appeal directly to your book's target audience. Your blog will be one of your most public arenas, so be certain that your "appearances" there support your overall marketing goals.

Marketing Through Your Site

With your site up and running, your next task is to find ways to use it as a marketing tool. More Web site visitors = more sales. Fortunately, the Web is all about marketing; you can choose from a number of ways for driving people to your Web site. The marketing techniques described in the following sections should help you get the best return from your online efforts.

Using Banner Ads

Banner ads are a common sight online. These graphic banners can contain animation, review quotes, cover art, and—always—a "click here" link to take readers to your Web site or online book sales portal. Do appropriate research to determine on which sites you would like to place your banner ads. The ads should appear on sites that cater to your target audience. If your book is about religion, your banner ads should appear on Web sites that cater to readers of religious information. If your book is a mystery, your banner ad should appear on sites that draw mystery lovers.

Most sites charge a "click-through" rate for banner ads, so you only pay for those readers who actually click the ad to access your book sales portal or Web site. Different sites and banner ads enjoy different click rates, but a click-through rate of 1 percent is considered great by many in the industry. Most sites charge by quantities of impressions or views, such as 1,000, 10,000, and so on. More popular sites charge higher rates than do sites with fewer visitors.

Unless you're a Web design professional, you should hire a banner ad design firm to create your banner ad. You need a professional to determine what kind of content will best represent your book *and* generate the highest reader response. In many cases, the sites on which you are advertising on will create the artwork for you at no charge. You have three options for placing your banner ad online:

~ You can contact individual sites yourself, review their advertising policies and rates, and choose the sites that best meet your book's target audience and your marketing budget.

~ You can hire an advertising agency to place the ads for you. Most agencies work only with large clients, but you might be able to locate an online advertising agency that specializes in advertisements for products within your book's genre or topic area. Search online for the appropriate agency, then do your research to understand specifically what services the agency will provide for you, and at what cost.

~ You can join a banner ad "network" or exchange, in which your banner ad is posted on the sites of other members of the network in exchange for posting their banner ads on your site. Again, do your research well; although networks and exchanges can save you time and money by finding the right venues for your banner ads and by placing appropriate ads on your site, you need to carefully determine that they'll do just that. Make sure you understand specifically what the service is offering before you agree to participate.

For your banner ad to be cost-effective, it will need to be well-designed and well-placed. Again, do your homework carefully so you know that the service you're contracting can provide the assistance you need at a price that fits within your marketing budget.

Marketing through E-mail Newsletters and E-zines

You can gather names for your e-mail newsletter mailings through your Web site. Adding interactive capabilities to your Web site, such as an e-mail contact link, links to book sales portals, and reader subscription lists is an absolute must if you want to draw repeat visitors and gain the most marketing value possible from your site. By providing readers with the ability to sign up for e-mail newsletters and other informational mailings, you can build a valuable e-mail contact list, and you can avoid regulatory issues that govern the use of e-mail and faxes for communicating promotional information without the express consent of the recipient (see "Creating an E-mail Opt-in List" later in this chapter).

E-mail newsletters and e-zines reach hundreds of thousands of readers every day. Like their print counterparts, most electronic newsletters and e-zines carry advertising for products of special interest to their readers. Some e-mail newsletters and e-zines enjoy large subscription lists, so they offer a powerful vehicle for getting your advertising message in front of a targeted readership. These venues can be useful for marketing both fiction and nonfiction books.

Again, check out the newsletter or e-zine carefully before committing to an advertising program. You want to be certain that the online publication is crafted to appeal to your targeted audience and that your book's advertisement will be a good "fit." Typically, you can buy advertising packages or pay for one-time-only advertisements.

You also might want to consider starting your own e-mail newsletter or e-zine to market your book. As with blogs, these electronic publications can offer a number of marketing opportunities. You can use your e-zine or newsletter to distribute press releases, announce upcoming appearances, highlight favorable reviews of your book, and to issue other alerts about your book. And you can carry your own advertisements free of charge within your newsletter or e-zine.

Running an E-mail Campaign

You can distribute your own e-mail newsletter and advertise your Web site—and your book—through your own e-mail marketing campaign. By compiling a contact list of potential readers, book buyers, journalists, organizations, and others who have a shared interest in your book's topic area or genre, you create a target group for periodic e-mail distributions.

Your e-mail campaign might involve distributing press releases, announcing upcoming speaking engagements, highlighting or linking to current events or articles on topics associated with your book. You might also use e-mail to distribute information about special promotions for your book, contests, seminars, and other marketing events. You can distribute e-mail newsletter and marketing messages yourself, or you can hire an e-mail marketing business to take care of the distributions for you. But *don't* simply put together a list of e-mail addresses and start blasting them with advertisements for your book—that's spamming, and it's annoying, counter-productive, and against the law.

Spamming is the term used to describe bulk-distributions of electronic sales information. Most federal, state, and local anti-spamming laws (many ISPs have anti-spamming rules) prohibit the use of fax machines and ISP addresses in the bulk distribution of advertising messages. When you send out messages that contain sales information—pricing information, links to purchase portals, and any other information that is designed solely to promote the sale of your book—you need to take care to avoid violating state and local anti-spamming laws.

Visit *www.spamlaws.com* to learn more about federal and state anti-spam legislation. The Privacy Rights Clearinghouse (*www.privacyrights.org*) is another reliable source for information regarding consumer rights and advertising.

Creating an E-mail Opt-in List

The development of a contact list is an essential part of creating a marketing campaign for your book. You'll use the contact list to distribute press releases, announcements of upcoming speaking engagements, book signings, appearances, awards, and other information associated with you and your book. Many, but not all, of these contacts might also wish to receive sales, marketing, and promotional information about your book. These individuals are likely candidates for your e-mail marketing list.

To be certain that your e-mail newsletter and/or marketing messages go out only to those individuals who want to receive them (and to avoid run-ins with anti-spam laws), you can create an *e-mail opt-in list.* These lists are, at their most basic form, subscription lists; by subscribing to your e-mail newsletter or update service, individuals or organizations give you express permission to contact them with sales and promotional information.

Opt-in lists take many forms, but the two most common are simple opt-in subscription forms and *confirmed opt-in* arrangements. Both of these lists begin when a visitor to your Web site completes an information form and chooses an option that states that he or she wishes to receive periodic information mailings from you. If you are creating a confirmed opt-in list, you reply with an e-mail verifying the subscriber's intent to join your service. By replying to your message, the individual verifies that the subscription was valid, and not added by a third party.

Sending Out E-mail Blasts

Take care in designing e-mail messages that will be engaging, interesting, and efficient. Keep your messages short, and remember to be honest in your characterization of their content. If you're billing information as news, make sure it really is news; send promotional and advertising messages only to recipients who have "opted in" to receive such mailings. E-mail "blasts" or mass mailings are an effective way to distribute such information, but you need to take care not to over-saturate your recipients with too many messages in too short a time period.

On average, e-mailings should go out no more than once a month. If you have a deadline-driven piece of information that warrants a follow-up announcement, you might occasionally send a mid-month mailing as well. But bombarding your recipients with multiple mailings in a short time period will annoy them and lessen the impact of the information you're distributing. It also increases the likelihood that they will ask you to remove them from your list. Put time and care into crafting this part of your campaign, if you decide to incorporate it into your Web marketing efforts.

Many services offer assistance in designing and executing e-mail marketing mailings. Companies such as Constant Contact (*www.constantcontact.com*) and Vertical Response (*www.verticalresponse.com*) manage e-mail subscriptions and newsletter distributions. (You can find other such agencies by searching under the terms 'e-mail marketing' or 'e-mail management' using any major search engine.) Most such companies offer free start-up packages, where the first twenty-five to fifty recipients are free, then charge a low monthly fee for continued e-mail campaign management. Your mailings will probably only need to reach 100-200 recipients, so costs should be manageable. Read the company's online information, check their client list, and speak with a representative for more information. Understand specifically what services the company provides, how you can use those services, and how the service charges are assessed.

Promoting Your Book through Other Online Avenues

In addition to writing and maintaining a blog, hosting a Web site, and sending out e-mail updates, you have a number of other options for promoting your book online. These include participating in chat rooms, joining Livejournal online communities, and podcasting; signing up for pay-per-click promotions through the Google and Yahoo! services; and participating in Amazon's Search Inside This Book™ feature.

Online Chat Rooms, Community Forums, and Podcasting

The ever-changing nature of electronic information continually opens up new avenues for marketing your book. With more of the world communicating more regularly through electronic messaging and broadcasts, your marketing campaign needs to explore and exploit as many of the available marketing venues as possible.

Chat rooms have been around for some time, but they're still a prime arena for reaching readers who share an interest in your book's topic or genre. By joining a chat room devoted to a subject related to your book's topic, you have an opportunity to gain valuable firsthand information about what other members of the chat room are reading, what events they're attending, and what news they're following. You also can post information about your book and your Web site in your own chat room messages. You can find and join chat rooms by searching online under your topic area and the terms "chat room," or by visiting Google, Yahoo!, or any major search engine and clicking the "Group" link.

Take the time to actively participate in chat rooms, rather than simply joining so you can post advertisements. Other members won't read—or appreciate—your use of the chat room as nothing more than a venue for posting free advertising.

Livejournal is a site devoted to the creation and ongoing maintenance of online "communities" devoted to a number of topics and areas of interest. The site describes itself as an "online journal service"; rather than hosting your own blog, you can simply create journal pages and post them to the forums of Livejournal community or communities to which you belong. These postings give you an opportunity to announce news and information about your book to a group of readers who have a demonstrated interest in your book's topic area. Your journal page can be added to multiple Livejournal community forums, thereby reaching an incredibly large readership. Simple membership is free, though you can buy paid membership with extended options. Visit *www.livejournal.com* to learn more.

Podcasting is a relatively new communication method that is rapidly gaining popularity. It involves creating and distributing a broadcast—a news update, announcement, or even a short "radio" program—to a list of broadcast subscribers. You record your message using special RDF XML technology to create a file that can be "read" by any digital audio player or computer with audio-playing software. You can create broadcasts about current events associated with your book's topic, announcements about your upcoming appearances and signings, reviews of other books within your genre or topic area, or any other type of news and information that will interest, entertain, or inform your book's target audience. Learn more about podcasting technology and techniques at the Wikepedia online dictionary (*www.wikepedia.org*) or at Indiepodder (*www.ipodder.org*). You can find directories of thousands of current podcasts at *www.podcast.net* (you can add your own directory here, as well).

Pay-Per-Click Advertising on Google and Yahoo!

The major search engine sites Google and Yahoo! both offer pay-per-click advertising opportunities that you can use to promote your book. In this form of advertising (also known as "search marketing"), you bid for specific keywords to be associated with your book. When a user visits the search engine and enters search terms including your keywords, your Web site is returned as a prominently displayed result for the search. Google has named its pay-per-click program AdWords; Yahoo!'s program is called Sponsored Search.

At both Google and Yahoo!, you bid for specific keywords or phrases. You need to choose carefully to be sure that the keywords you purchase the rights to are likely to appear in common searches by your target audience. At the same time, you need to choose terms that are unique to your book. If your book is historical fiction taking place in Charleston, South Carolina during the Civil War, for example, you might want to bid on "Civil War Charleston" or "antebellum Charleston." You would not, however, be wise to bid on words like "fiction" or "book"; if you do, you'll receive thousands of clicks from visitors with no interest in your book. Because of its ability to specifically target search results, this type of advertising is particularly useful for books with unique subject matter, nonfiction titles, historical fiction, and other books with narrow niche audiences.

As the name suggests, you are charged each time a searcher clicks on your link in the search results list. With thousands of potential visitors, the rewards—and the costs—of this type of marketing can be quite high. Don't allow expenses in these programs to become prohibitive; $50 a month should be the limit for most fiction or nonfiction books. Both Google and Yahoo! have monthly budgeting schemes that enable you to limit the total possible cost of your pay-per-click campaign. Visit their sites for more information.

Amazon's "Search Inside!™" Program

Another valuable way for driving readers to your book sales portal is Amazon's "Search Inside This Book" program. With this program, visitors to *Amazon.com* can search for books based on words or phrases contained within the book—in addition to searching based on author, title, and keywords. This program helps guarantee that potential readers who search Amazon for books like yours will find *your* book.

In addition to finding your book, visitors can preview a limited number of pages within your book, including the cover, table of contents, and the first chapter. Amazon has reported that books sold through their Web site that participate in the "Search Inside This Book" program have a 7 percent increase in sales over books that are not in the program.

Joining the program is relatively simple; you sign up on line at the Amazon site, and receive in return instructions for submitting a copy of your book (in printed, not electronic, format) to Amazon. In most cases, your book is entered into the system within five to seven weeks. Visit *www.amazon. com* for more details.

Setting up Reciprocal Links

Finally, don't overlook the value of setting up reciprocal links on your site to help increase site traffic and gain greater recognition for your book. You set up reciprocal links simply by agreeing to post links to other Web sites on your site; in return, those sites also include a link to your own Web site. In addition to offering links to other sites, you can set up reciprocal arrangements for book reviews and other book listings with authors and publishers working within your topic area.

Reciprocal links are a valuable tool for marketing your Web site and your book. Every visitor to a site with which you have a reciprocal agreement has an opportunity to learn of your site and to go there at the click of a link. Your site gets increased exposure through Internet searches, as well, since it will be returned as a result on any search that also returns any of your reciprocal partners as a result. Further, search engines check the number of links to your site when determining rankings; the more links to your site, the more important the search engines assume your site to be, and therefore, the higher the engines rank your site within search results.

Typically, you should make reciprocal agreements with sites that appeal to your targeted audience. As you identify the sites you'd most like to exchange links with, contact the sites' Webmasters for more information about forming a reciprocal arrangement.

Selling On Your Site

Although your Web site offers multiple opportunities for selling your book, you probably should not engage directly in e-commerce. In other words, unless you are an experienced online business owner, you should not sell books directly from your site. Doing so requires that you handle financial transactions, shipping, and other details that are difficult, time-consuming, and potentially risky for both you and your site visitors.

You can, however, link to sales portals for your book. These can include links to the AuthorHouse Bookstore listing for your book. AuthorHouse can then handle and track the sales transaction for you. Your Web site also can contain links directly to other book sales portals, including Amazon and Barnes & Noble.

Selling on Third-Party Sites

You also can sell your book by placing a link to your book's sales portals directly on third-party sites. This marketing technique is particularly effective for books with very genre-specific or otherwise uniquely specified target markets. Cookbooks, books on genealogy, local businesses, or history, hobbies and collections, and so on, are prime examples of publications that are well-suited to sales from third-party sites.

To effectively use this technique, you must first identify Web sites that are particularly effective for reaching your target audience. Each site's owner or Webmaster can then work out the arrangements for placing a link to your book's listing on an online sales portal such as the AuthorHouse Bookstore, Amazon, or Barnes & Noble. Some sites charge Web site royalties or other fees for such links; if that's the case, carefully review the agreement before signing.

Chapter 3

Public Relations

No matter how great your distribution channels are, your book won't sell if the public doesn't know it's available. Even if you've never thought of yourself as a "PR" person, you'll be amazed at how easily you can take on that role in the process of marketing your book. As the author, you are uniquely qualified to tell others about your book.

Publicizing your book is largely a process of catching the public's attention through the media. You must generate news about your book and learn how to use the media to get that news before the public. You need to develop skills in crafting newsworthy media releases, forming media contacts, and managing those contacts effectively. You also need to be committed to an ongoing public relations campaign; persistence is your greatest tool in this effort.

Using Press Releases and Media Kits

Press releases, also known as news releases, are one of the most effective ways to capture the public's attention. The best press releases are short, simple, and effective. These one-page announcements of newsworthy events associated with your book can be sent by themselves, with a review copy of your book, or as part of a larger media kit.

Writing a good press release takes some understanding of how and when the release is to be distributed. It also requires a keen editorial eye and a strong understanding of the market served by the media outlet receiving the release. Here, you learn how to craft an attention-grabbing press release and use it most effectively. You also learn how to put together a full media kit for any media outlet.

Understanding How Press Releases Work

You use press releases to generate publicity for your book. By sending notices to the media about your book's release, your speaking engagements, author signings, and other events associated with your book's publication and distribution, you provide news sources with the information and materials they need to keep your book before the public eye. Your press release may foster contacts from the media, reviews of your book, and requests for interviews.

A press release is news, however, not an advertisement. You must be sure, therefore, to build your release around a newsworthy event. Here are just some of the reasons for sending out a press release about your book:

~ To announce the release of your book

~ To highlight the relevance of your book's topic to a recent, controversial, or otherwise newsworthy event

~ To announce your appearance at a major event (local or state fair, community gathering, writing seminar, book reading/signing, etc.)

~ To announce articles published by or about you

~ To announce sales promotions, the availability of free samples, or upcoming demonstrations you'll be offering in relation to your book

~ To announce that you're starting a newsletter or e-zine

~ To announce the launch of your own Web site or online service

~ To announce that you're offering a class, seminar, or workshop

~ To announce an upcoming appearance on radio or television, or the publication of an in-print interview

~ To announce upcoming holiday events or programs with tie-ins to your book's topic

~ To announce the anniversary of your book's release date or a sales milestone

~ To announce your book's appearance on a bestseller list

~ To announce your book's winning of an award

Writing an Effective Press Release

You don't have to be a great journalist to put together a powerful press release. The most important rule is to keep it simple. Press releases should follow a basic Associated Press style; they tell the reader the "who, what, where, when, and why" of a newsworthy event associated with your book, and present that information in an "inverted pyramid" style. That simply means that the most important information—the basis for the entire press release—appears at the beginning of the release, and the remaining information diminishes in importance as it moves down the page.

Formatting Your News Release

Some media outlets receive hundreds (even thousands) of press releases each day, so it's important that your press release is easy to read, complete, and compelling. Using the right format is a critical first step in this process. The press release should contain no more than one double-spaced page of information that includes these major elements:

~ A boldly formatted line reading <u>***FOR IMMEDIATE RELEASE***</u>, which lets the media outlet know the information can be published as soon as it's received

~ Contact information for more information, including name, phone, e-mail, and fax details

~ An attention-catching headline

~ The city and state from which you're releasing the news, followed by the first and most important information the release is conveying

~ Two or three additional paragraphs of text that provide the remaining information for your release

~ A final paragraph that provides a brief author bio or information about the publishing company distributing your book

~ Three pound signs (###), centered below your final paragraph, to indicate the end of the document

Writing Great Content

When determining what content to include in your release, remember that you are conveying *news* associated with you and your book. Your headline should powerfully and immediately announce that news:

"*Food for Thought* Author Discusses Controversial Animal Rights Issues at Upcoming Seminar"

"'Holiday in the Park' Festival to Include Book Signing by Local Author"

"*Money in Your Pocket* Author Gene Willard Takes Financial Advice Online"

"Local Fitness Author Encourages City Workers to Be Big-Time Losers"

Your headline's goal is to catch the reporter's eye and draw it down to your opening paragraph. It should give the reader an accurate heads-up about content, but it's a taste of the news to come, not the whole story.

Your first paragraph should concisely state the important facts of your press release. Who and what the release is about, when and where the associated event took place (is taking place or will take place), and why the event is worth knowing about or participating in. Be sure to describe your book in this first important paragraph of text.

The next few paragraphs should offer important ideas and information that expand upon those basic details. The final paragraph of the news release should include a brief author bio and, if appropriate, information about the book's publisher or distributor. Remember that your press release will be used to generate news, but it won't necessarily be reprinted word for word.

Remember, that each press release is relating news about a single event associated with you and your book. Keep the content of the release focused and concise, and offer some information that's truly useful for the media outlet you're contacting. Here are some other important tips for writing great press releases:

~ Remember that you're writing for editors, so be clear, concise, and *accurate*. Check spelling, dates, and details carefully.

~ Include your book's Web site address along with other contact information for arranging interviews or requesting review copies.

~ Don't use boxes, pictures, or other graphic elements in the document; these things tie up fax machines and consume ink, which will irk many editors. Overly "designed" documents will also look like ads, and might be tossed out without a further glance.

~ Don't include pricing or ordering information; your press release cannot be worded as a solicitation piece (you'll read more about this later).

~ Don't embellish your piece with overblown hype and worn clichés such as "a must read" or "soon-to-be-bestseller."

~ Don't bill your release as groundbreaking news unless it is groundbreaking.

Writing Press Releases for Online Media Outlets

The Web is one of the world's most commonly used research tools. Journalists search the Web regularly, for article research as well as for news releases. As many as 60 percent of people with online access use the Web to find news, and nearly all journalists go online every day. Therefore, you're wise to incorporate Web news sources in your public relations efforts by sending selected sites copies of appropriate press releases.

When customizing your press releases for use online, remember that most people will find your information as the result of an online search. Therefore, you'll want to be sure your press release contains terms that are likely to come up in searches conducted by people interested in your book and its topic. Although your press release should be structured with the same "inverted pyramid" form and directed content advised for releases targeting other media outlets, be sure to use as many "searchable" terms as possible in the body and headline of your document.

Putting Together a Press or Media Kit

You'll want to include relevant press releases in all of your *media kits*. These kits are collections of material about you and your book which you bundle and send to representatives of the media. The media kit should promote both you and your book by including news, marketing materials, and background information. A typical media kit might include:

~   A cover letter, personalized for the recipient. Your cover letter should introduce you and your book and very briefly explain the purpose of this contact; you might be writing to ask for a book review or to arrange for an interview, for example. Your cover letter should specifically highlight the unique benefit of your book for readers and for the audience of the media outlet you're contacting. You can supplement this with a personalized Post-it note with a short, personal message to the recipient, stuck in a conspicuous place in or on the kit.

~ Relevant press releases and press clippings about you and your book. If you've published articles or interviews, be certain to include copies of those as well.

~ An author bio sheet that contains interesting and engaging information about your background and experiences; again, you can customize this information to appeal to specific markets.

~ Sample questions and answers, particularly if you're writing to request an interview about your book.

~ A fact sheet about your book that lists its basic information, including the book's title, publisher, ISBN number, page count, publication date, and price.

~ Flyers, bookmarks, clipsheets of artwork from the book, or other marketing materials used to promote your book.

~ A schedule of appearances, book signings, and events.

~ Author portrait photo or photos taken of you during appearances at events.

~ Review copy of your book, when appropriate; otherwise, a sample chapter or excerpt, along with cover art. Only send review copies to contacts that can result in news stories or other media coverage. Sending review copies to bookstores, libraries, schools, and other non-media sources won't generate media coverage, and therefore isn't an efficient use of your marketing resources.

~ If you aren't certain the recipient will be interested in a review copy of your book, you instead can include a review copy request card; recipients can return the card to you or call the number on the card to request a review copy of your book.

As you collect news clippings and quotes about your book, you can copy these and include them in your media kit. Put your kit in a simple but nice folder, and pack the information in a way that makes the material easy to look through and the smaller marketing pieces easy to find. And again, be prepared to customize the contents of your media kit to match the market into which you're sending it.

Creating Media Lists and Contacts

A good media contact list contains more than names and addresses of media outlets. Notes about the media markets, target audience, types of coverage, publication schedule, editor/reporter/producer names, and so on will help you plan and compose your contacts to have the most impact. Remember to start small for the most effective launch of your marketing campaign. Concentrate on local and regional media first.

Researching the Media for Your Market

Begin by researching the media you want to reach, to determine what types of news they typically cover. Read back issues of publications—either online or in the periodicals section of your library—to determine which print media outlets cover stories related to your book's topic. If the source typically covers books, what kinds of books do they feature and does their coverage tend to focus on authors, content, sales, or other book-related issues? Listen to radio programs and watch television programs before contacting their representatives; your contact should reflect a basic understanding of the types of issues and events covered by their programs. Your cover letter and media kit should be put together to present your book from the angle most likely to fit with the outlet's typical coverage content and style.

Different types of media may be interested in specific types of stories. Most outlets are interested in carrying human interest stories, news related to timely or topical events, stories with a unique "angle," and stories tied to local interests or events. Radio producers are drawn to topics that will drive debate and discussion, such as issues with social or political implications. The better you understand the market, the better your chances of being covered by it.

Working with Newspapers and Magazines

Local newspapers are a particularly important source for targeting your local market in the beginning stages of your marketing campaign. Daily newspapers run on tight deadlines, so you'll need to time your contacts carefully. The reporters who work at daily newspapers typically get stories out within twenty-four to forty-eight hours, but feature writers have longer lead times, and usually start working on features weeks in advance of their publication dates. Keep this in mind when you're tying your book's publicity to a holiday or special event in your area, and time the receipt of your press releases, media kits, or other contact to accommodate these schedules.

Magazines are great venues for publicizing your book because they target specific audiences and thus make it easier for you to reach your own market. Magazine feature articles and book reviews tend to be very thorough, and they speak directly to the magazine readers; these qualities work to make most magazine pieces great vehicles for publicizing your book. Getting a review or article published in major magazines can be difficult, however. You'll need to research your market *and* this medium carefully, to target magazines that are likely to be interested in covering your book and whose publication schedule works best with your campaign. Don't bother targeting national weekly magazines in your media campaign; national weeklies rarely publish articles on mainstream books, and then do so only *after* the books have gained major national attention.

Again, be sure your contact coincides with the magazine's publishing schedule. Most monthly magazine writers work at least two months in advance of the publication date for their piece—even further in advance for stories linked to major holidays or events. If you want your publicity to appear in association with a guest appearance, speaking engagement, publication date, holiday, or other critical time, be sure that your contact gives the magazine reporter ample lead time.

Pitching your book to the reporter of any publication requires planning and preparation. Be sure that you can quickly convey to the media contact precisely why your book is important to the media outlet's audience and what real benefit it offers them. Be concise, clear, and complete. Practice your pitch call with a friend or associate, and have others review your pitch letters.

Using Radio and Television in Your Campaign

Although coverage on nationally syndicated programs is out of reach for most first-time authors, locally produced programs can offer real opportunities for reaching local—and even regional—audiences. Often, radio and locally broadcast television programs are willing to broadcast short special-interest bits about books or even feature authors in short on-air interviews or call-in programs. This coverage can also mention author Web sites and offer other information about how to purchase books.

Radio is a great venue for promoting how-to books, political books, and stories that have strong local interest. Again, know the station's program list and audience demographics, and tailor your contact to fit closely with this "profile."

Those living in small or rural areas can actually make better use of television marketing than can those in major metropolitan areas such as New York, Chicago, and Los Angeles. Local broadcasting stations and public access channels typically are anxious to broadcast stories of local interest.

Again, the more closely you can tie news associated with your book—public appearances, author signings, festival booths, and so on—with local events, the better your chance of getting television coverage. Holding an event such as a reading, workshop, or seminar, and publicizing it often can get local television coverage when a simple book release announcement won't. Consider the types of programming carried by local stations and target your contact with those stations accordingly.

Adding Web Sites and Newsletters to Your Contact List

Don't underestimate the value of publicizing news in newsletters and on Web sites. Hundreds of thousands of newsletters are published in the United States each year, and each of them targets a very specific readership. Readers know that newsletter content is aimed specifically at their needs and interests, and therefore are likely to give at least cursory attention to most articles and reports appearing in newsletters they subscribe to.

You can distribute your news releases through professional services such as the free service PR Web (*www.prweb.com*) and the paid service PR Newswire (*www.prnewswire.com*). These services will forward your press releases to a number of online news services; many journalists use the services to receive regular "feeds" of news releases. Visit the sites for more information on creating and submitting press releases through their services.

Your own online research will also reveal a number of relevant blogs, online journals, and other Web publications that can also be effective outlets for your online news releases. Again, research the market carefully and be certain your contact is customized to match the readership and typical content for the online outlet you're contacting.

Following Protocols for Contacting the Media

Media contacts take the form of mailings, faxes, e-mails, and phone contacts. Some basic protocols apply to all media contacts, but these different forms of media contact also have some unique rules of their own.

Contacting by Phone

Personal contact with reporters and editors is a great way to forge stronger relationships with the media, but it requires some finesse and fine-tuned management. Follow a few basic rules for phone contacts:

~ Don't call a reporter or editor to tell them you're going to send them a media kit, news release, fax, or e-mail. They receive hundreds of these contacts daily, so your call to announce the arrival of yet another media piece won't be welcomed by a busy reporter or editor.

~ Workers at daily newspapers are always busiest in the morning, so you're unlikely to make personal contact with reporters there before noon. Morning calls are more likely to simply annoy the editor or reporter and damage what might have been a valuable contact.

~ Practice what you want to say ahead of time; write down what you want to say and read it out loud until you feel comfortable that you've "learned" your script.

~ Learn to wind your way through the "layers" of personnel within the media outlet to reach the appropriate contact. Don't be hostile with the receptionist or administrative assistants you encounter; simply tell them who you are and what you're calling about, and ask them who you should speak with. Be pleasant *and* persistent.

~ Persistence is critical, but don't slip into the realm of harassment. You can count on being directed to voice mail; leave a brief, but complete message (again, practice ahead of time). If you've left two or three messages and receive no reply, accept that the editor or reporter isn't interested in following up on this contact, and move on.

~ Keep a record of the calls that you've made, including the media outlet, individual you've contacted there, and the date and time of your contact. Note the nature of your contact, as well, including its purpose and content. This information will prevent you from duplicating contacts and will be a handy reference if you receive a follow up call or contact.

~ If you hit a brick wall, don't take it personally. Your ability to focus on the work ahead rather than past disappointments is critical to keeping your public relations work positive and on track.

Faxing Media Outlets

Faxing is an efficient way to submit a single news release to selected media outlets, but *spamming* media outlets with advertising faxes sent to a bulk mailing list is not only annoying and counterproductive, it's illegal. According to federal law, using a fax machine to advertise a product, good, or service is illegal, unless you have the express written permission of the recipient prior to sending the fax. As we mentioned earlier, any notice you send out that contains pricing or ordering information is considered an advertisement. Sending a fax to an agency or individual that has requested that you stop sending faxes to their number is also a violation of federal law. Finally, faxing news to retailers or private individuals is also considered advertising, and is therefore illegal; news releases can only be sent to appropriate media outlets.

For all of these reasons, you must carefully consider the wisdom of sending a news release via fax to *anyone*. If you do fax a news release to an appropriate news outlet, follow our previous advice and keep the release to a single page of double-spaced type with no text boxes, illustrations, or other graphics that will tie up the fax machine and use excessive toner.

> You should know the law regarding fax and e-mail spam. To learn more, visit *www.privacyrights.org*.

E-mailing Media Contacts

Although many editors and reporters accept contacts through e-mail, it's another potentially damaging form of contact to incorporate in your public relations campaign. The same rules against spamming that we've just mentioned in relationship to faxing apply to e-mail. Many media outlets will not accept or open e-mail attachments, to avoid the danger of computer viruses.

We don't recommend that you e-mail numerous media outlets as part of your general public relations efforts. If you do decide to send news releases via e-mail, follow the formatting advice offered earlier and send the text of your news release directly in the e-mail message itself. Use an informative subject line, so the recipient immediately understands the nature of your message. And make sure you do a virus scan of your press release file before you send it. The last thing you want to do is inadvertently infect a reporter's computer with a virus.

And again—do NOT send pricing and ordering information or any other content that could be perceived as advertising. Don't e-mail individuals or retailers, either, and make a note to cease all e-mails to individuals or agencies that ask you to take them from your contact list.

AuthorHouse asks that you remove its contact information from any fax or e-mail that you send to *anyone*. If you do decide to send news releases to media outlets via fax or within e-mail messages, please be sure that the contact information on the document lists only your own contact data (your name and telephone number at a minimum).

Following Up on Media Contacts

Sending out news releases and media kits isn't the most important phase of your public relations campaign; following up on those initial contacts is absolutely critical to success. Authors who follow up with the media have much more success publicizing their books than do those authors who fail to follow up.

Fielding Follow-up Requests from the Media

Follow-up calls from editors and reporters might come immediately, or as much as three weeks after you distribute your publicity piece, but you cannot predict when or if you'll receive the calls. Again, practice your conversation by anticipating and preparing to answer the types of questions the reporter or editor might ask. If the caller requests a review copy, send it right away, then follow up within a week to see if he or she has additional questions or would like to schedule an interview.

Making Your Own Follow-up Calls

Although a reporter or editor might follow up with you after receiving your release or kit, more frequently you will need to follow up with them. Again, time your call to match the media outlet's schedule. Be pleasant and direct, as you work your way through the phone system to the individual you need to speak with.

When you reach the editor or reporter to whom you've directed your news pieces, DO NOT ask whether he or she received your news release. This pointless question is an annoying waste of the editor's time, and typically he or she will say "no," then hang up. Instead, tell the editor who you are and that you sent them a news release related to your book; explain that you are calling to offer your assistance in providing further information for their use in crafting a story about the piece, writing a review, or scheduling an interview. You also can remind the editor that you will happily send him or her a free review copy of your book. If you've scheduled an appearance, book signing, or other event subsequent to sending the release, you can mention that as well.

Again, be pleasant, direct, helpful, and willing to answer questions. If the reporter brushes you off, remain pleasant, say good-bye, and move on to the next contact. Keep your contacts pleasant and upbeat so that you can continue to try to forge a working relationship with the majority of contacts on your media list.

Conducting Interviews

If you land an interview in response to your public relations efforts, congratulations! Print and broadcast interviews can be powerful publicity machines for promoting your book. But talking to members of the media can seem overwhelming, especially when you're in the beginning stages of your public relations efforts. The important thing to remember is that the interview is designed to gather information about things you know very, very well— your book and your background. With some preparation and practice, you can learn to gain the most from media interviews.

Preparing for the Interview

When you put together your media kit, you probably created a sample question-and-answer sheet. The items you recorded there will give you a strong head start in preparing to handle media interviews. Here are some subjects you should prepare to discuss in your interview:

~ Your background, and how your other interests, ideas, or expertise evolved into the writing of your book

~ How you came up with the idea for your book

~ Some of the more interesting ways you researched or learned of the information you used when writing the book

~ How your book connects with local interests

~ Authors or books that have inspired or influenced you and your work

Again, research is a critical key to this phase of preparation. Read, watch, and listen to interviews with the media outlets you're contacting. Become familiar with the interview format, the types of questions typically asked, and the length of time slotted for responses. Learn which types of issues associated with your book are most likely to resonate with the media outlet's audience.

Practice answering those questions. Interview yourself; sit in a chair before a large mirror and run through your interview questions and answers. After you've become comfortable with these self-interviews, enlist the aid of a friend, relative, or your spouse as a partner in practice interviews. Give your partner your list of interview Q&As, but tell them to feel free to improvise as well.

Handling the Actual Interview

Most interviews will be arranged in advance. If the interview will be conducted over the phone, be sure that you arrange to take the call in a quiet place where you won't be distracted or interrupted. Also, be sure to have practiced your interviews in this environment, too, so you feel more prepared and comfortable during the actual call.

Listen to the question, carefully think through the appropriate response, then clearly and carefully relay your response to the interviewer. Though you need to be concise and efficient, you don't need to rush. Take your time, remember the talking points you've practiced, and answer questions in a way that presents you and your book in the most positive and interesting light for the individual media outlet's audience. With practice, you'll also learn to relax during interviews, which will also help make you more effective.

The more often you practice responding to questions about your book, the better able you'll be to say the things you *really* want to say. And that's an important point; don't say ANYTHING to an interviewer that you don't want broadcast to the public. Even if the interviewer assures you repeatedly that your comment is "off the record," it won't be. If you say it to a reporter, it's public knowledge—period. So think *carefully* before you respond to questions.

If you feel yourself becoming shaken and nervous, take a deep breath and give yourself a few seconds to collect your thoughts. If you are asked a question that you don't know the answer to, tell the reporter that you'll have to consider the question and get back to them. You'll be less nervous as you gain more experience; again, practice is the key.

Finally, remember that the best way to avoid "mis-statements" is to be honest. Don't exaggerate or spout overblown hype about your book. And don't stress out over mistakes; everyone slips up at times, and you'll improve with experience.

Following Up After the Interview

Within a day or two of the interview, phone or e-mail the reporter, editor, or producer who interviewed you, to be certain that they have all of the information they need to complete their piece. They may have developed more questions in the course of preparing their story or broadcast, or they may need more information on one of the interview points. Remember to thank them for their time.

Chapter 4

Book Signings and Author Tours

As your book's publicist, your first goal is to make sure that people know about your book and are encouraged to buy it. Personal appearances and book signings are excellent ways to accomplish both goals. By speaking directly to your potential buyers, you give your book a human "face"; you have an opportunity to interact directly with the public; and your would-be readers have an opportunity to connect with you, your book, and its message. Book signings and author tours are a primary source of publicity—and sales.

Acquiring and Hosting a Book Signing

Book signings require some careful planning and hard work. To plan for and conduct a successful book signing, you need to:

~ Research likely venues and locales

~ Contact appropriate individuals at each locale and arrange for the book signing event

~ Schedule the book signing to coincide (and not clash) with other area events

~ Gather materials and prepare for the book signing

~ In some cases, order books to fulfill the sales opportunity

~ Take care of the signing set-up, presentation, and clean-up

~ Follow up with contacts after the book signing.

Researching in Advance of Your Book Signing

Research is as critical for planning a successful book signing, as it is for every phase of your promotional and marketing plan. Your goal in conducting a book signing is twofold:

~ To draw people to the event

~ To sell books

To reach either goal, you need to find the best venues for your book signing, and then plan a book signing event that's sure to succeed with the crowd you attract to each venue.

Notice that we use the term "venue" here, rather than "bookstore." Yes, bookstores are logical places to conduct an author appearance and book signing; but they aren't the *only* locations you should consider. Book clubs, professional and social organization meetings, and retail outlets associated with your book's topic are all good venues for conducting a book signing. This is another case where starting small in your marketing efforts pays off. By focusing your first attempts at organizing a book signing in local venues, you'll have a better chance to scout the area for potential locations, and then to research those locations to determine what type of publicity and presentation will work best.

You also need to research the area's other events to determine the best schedule for your author signing. You don't want to conflict with other major events in the area. Read the local newspapers and check with area educational and professional organizations to determine what other events are scheduled to occur in your area. Although large festivals and gatherings will hurt attendance at a conflicting small book signing event, you might be able to schedule a signing to "piggyback" on the success of a larger, well-established event. You can, for example, schedule your book signing to occur in the days following a major festival or gathering, then "work the crowds" at the larger event, handing out brochures and announcements about your upcoming appearance.

Based on your research, create a contact list of potential venues. Contact the store, organization, or locale to get the name of the manager or event coordinator you'll need to work with to schedule a book signing. Go to the locales to get a feel for the space and to gain a sense of what type of presentation might work best with the location's clientele or membership. Get on the locale's events mailing list to find out what kinds of activities and events are hosted there.

With your research in place, contact the locale and ask to speak to the person you've identified as your primary contact there. Introduce yourself and your book, and explain that you'd like to arrange for a book signing event at their location. Be sure to explain that you're a local author, as most small venues are more interested in promoting local talent. Be sure to ask what they most want to achieve from the book signing event. Be prepared to incorporate their goals into your plans, but come with ideas of your own as well.

Send your contact a copy of your media kit, being sure to include press releases, bookmarks, promotional photos, and other marketing materials, along with a sample copy of your book. Also, be prepared to talk about how you can assist in publicizing the event. Your goal—and, in most cases, the goal of the venue contact—is to draw *more* people to the locale for your book signing than might otherwise be there. Be sure to convey your willingness to do whatever you can to help publicize the event, so you can attain that goal.

Scheduling and Promoting the Book Signing

As with any event, timing is important for a successful book signing. Although your contacts will have advice and ideas for the best scheduling within their individual locale, you also need to give thought to how your book signing will coincide with other area festivals, gatherings, and events.

When the event is scheduled, plan (in consultation with your venue contact) your promotional campaign. Distribute a press release announcing the book signing to all local radio, television, newspapers, and other local news outlets. Create flyers or posters, and distribute them to local businesses, retail outlets, libraries, university student information areas, and other gathering spots. (ALWAYS ask permission before posting a notice or leaving brochures in any location.) Be sure to list your book signing in the local newspaper's events column, and try to acquire an interview or article about you and your book to appear in the paper in the days preceding the book signing. If possible, arrange for the newspaper to send someone to cover the event.

Ask the store or other venue whether they'll be sending out a notification of your book signing in their newsletter or other promotional mailing, and offer to contribute any names you might have to their mailing list. Find out what kinds of advertising the venue prefers, and how you can best help them carry out those activities. And don't hesitate to promote the book signing to your family and friends as well. Make sure that the people you know are aware of the event, and ask them to come and bring a friend. You can't be shy about promoting your book; the more people who attend your book signing, the better chance for its success. Bookstores notice when an author signing has drawn a large crowd, and are more likely to stock that author's books.

Many authors send out invitations to their book signings, and report that this simple step increases the turnout. Sending traditional invitations requires a relatively low investment in both time and money, but you also can use an electronic invitation service, such as evite (*www.evite.com*). You can use the service to send online invitations to anyone on your list with an e-mail address; the service is free and it even gives you the option of sending a reminder notice as the date approaches.

Plan an event—not just a book signing. Based on your research, you should know the space you'll be working in, and the size and interests of the crowd that you might draw. If you're promoting a cookbook, consider hosting a cooking demonstration with a follow-up book signing. If you've written a book of historical fiction, consider coming dressed in period costume. Readings and demonstrations are just some of the things you can do to make your book signing more enjoyable and more attractive to an audience. Be sure to mention the event on your promotional flyers, press releases, and other event publicity, so readers know you're offering more than just an opportunity to buy a signed copy of your book.

Preparing for Your Book Signing

Beyond specific props that you might need for a special demonstration, workshop, or performance, be sure to come to the book signing with all necessary promotional materials, equipment, and supplies. Most importantly, be certain that an ample supply of books will be on hand. This may require that you purchase and bring the books yourself. If your book signing is in a bookstore, your contact there might be able to help you predict how many copies you should have on hand; in most cases, plan on taking at least thirty copies of your book. You also need to have a generous supply of bookmarks, brochures, promotional photos, and other free promotional materials to hand out. You should also come with marketing materials that tell people how to order your book, should you sell out of your available copies.

Your research in advance of the presentation should prepare you for the equipment you'll need as well. If you need to bring your own table and chair, your own book easels, and perhaps a presentation board, you need to know that in advance. If you intend to gather names and contact information for promotional mailings, take along the cards you'll use to gather that data. You'll want to have a good supply of pens available as well.

If you can arrange for a friend to take pictures during the event, you can then use those photographs in later promotional packages. If the local newspaper sends a photographer, ask that person for a copy of his or her photos, so you can have reproductions made.

Order promotional materials and book copies well in advance. If your signing is in a bookstore, make arrangements in advance for handling payment for copies you bring to the store, versus those the store will have in stock. If you are selling the books yourself, make sure you have the ability to make change. Finally, create a list of the items you'll take to the signing, and make sure that all items are gathered up and ready to go the day before the event.

Conducting a Successful Book Signing

On the day of your book signing, you'll be grateful for all of your advance preparation. The better prepared you are, the less chance you have of forgetting or losing some "must-have" item, and arriving at the event late, exhausted, and frazzled. Be prepared to enjoy yourself! If you have fun, the audience will, too.

Arrange a good arrival time with your contact at the venue; typically, a few hours gives you time to set up your book signing area, with time left over to relax, circulate throughout the location a bit, and prepare yourself mentally for the event. Be sure to stock your table with plenty of your promotional materials; bookmarks, brochures, note pads or other giveaways, raffle cards, and other items should be handy and easily accessible to passersby. If you've taken a poster, display it on a nearby easel, and place another copy (with your host's permission) in the window or lobby. Get the names of anyone who helps you with your set-up, so you can thank them personally when you follow up after the event.

If you have time before the event begins, circulate throughout the locale, handing out bookmarks or other promotional materials and inviting people to come visit your book signing event. Be happy, be positive, and let people know you're glad to be there. If people are passing by, invite them to take the materials you have available. Thank everyone who buys a book, and be sure to place a bookmark or flyer in each copy you sell. That puts more of your marketing materials in circulation.

Finally, don't become discouraged if you find that you haven't drawn much of a crowd. Don't sit behind your table and wait for people to come to you—get up and work the room! Take copies of your book around and ask people if they'd like to leaf through it. If you're in a bookstore, go to the section that sells books on your topic or genre, and strike up conversations with the shoppers in those sections. Invite them to your presentation, or ask them to leaf through a copy of your book and let you know what they think. Afterward, you can use the experience to determine what you might have done to help make the event more successful.

After the event is over, make sure your area is clean and in good order before you leave. Thank the people who attended the event before they leave, but also remember to thank the people who worked with you at the venue for their time and effort. Again, make sure you have their names, so you can send them a follow-up thank-you note as well. Finally, if you have copies of your book left over, ask your contact if you can leave some signed copies with them for sale in the days to come.

Following Up After the Signing

Within a few days of the event, place a follow-up call or e-mail to your contact to gather their feedback about the event. Also, ask if they need more copies of your book. Finally, check with them about scheduling future book signings or events, or whether they have other locations where you might appear. And don't forget to send a thank-you note to the manager of the location, as well as to any people there who helped you during the event.

Scheduling Author Tours

Author tours are a series of appearances and events that you undertake to publicize your book in multiple locations and venues. Your tour might take you around the city or around the world, depending upon your book's topic, and your marketing goals and budget. Typically, author tours involve interviews, public readings, book signings, demonstrations, workshops, speaking engagements, and other book-related events. As with any marketing activity, start small; local events and locations typically are most interested in promoting a regional author's work.

Planning Your "Stops" and Arranging Events

To organize an author tour, you must first research the locales you want to include in the tour to determine the kinds of venues and events available for your appearances and participation. As with book signings, you aren't just interested in identifying bookstores; you'll want to look for local community festivals, libraries, educational programs (schools, colleges, and universities), book clubs, specialty shops, and retail outlets associated with your book's topic, and other potential venues for discussing your book or presenting demonstrations based on its content. You'll also want to research local newspapers, radio, and television stations, to determine what opportunities exist for reviews and interviews.

Based on the sites you locate, determine what kind of event you could conduct there that would be the most likely to have a good turnout. Your author tour might include a variety of activities, tailored to the tour's stops. Read community events calendars and talk to local event organizers to get a sense of what types of events typically are offered in the area, how those events are organized and advertised, and which types of events tend to draw the biggest crowds.

When you've compiled a list of potential "stops" on your tour, begin contacting the owners, organizers, managers, or events coordinators associated with each venue. You should begin making these contacts no later than two months before you plan to begin your tour. Present your ideas for your appearance, and ask your contacts how you might assist in publicizing the event. Send a media kit to appropriate contacts at each site, addressed specifically to the events coordinator, manager, or other individual with whom you'll work to schedule and organize your author event. Just be certain to coordinate your publicity efforts with the appropriate representative at each event, so you aren't duplicating or overlooking essential tasks. Your goal is to draw *more* public attention and traffic to the locale, rather than just capitalizing on the crowd that would be there with or without your presence.

Gathering Materials and Organizing Your Travel

As when planning for a book signing, you'll need to plan for all of the materials and supplies you'll need on your tour. Unlike a signing, however, you need to plan to have these materials on hand at a number of locations and for multiple dates. Again, plan what you'll need, based on your events, and then be prepared to have all of those materials with you at each location.

You might want to consider holding a drawing for a free autographed copy of your book. Use "sign up" cards to gather audience names and contact information; you can use the completed cards for the drawing, and to compile a list for future promotional mailings. If you plan such a drawing, be sure to have plenty of cards available for distributing at each stop along your tour.

Put together a tour "log," in which you record all of the essential information for each stop on your tour; location, address, contact name, publicity schedule, materials/ supplies necessary for the event, accommodation and travel arrangements, and so on. If possible, leave space for recording notes after the event as well. There, you can note necessary follow-up and stocking information, as well as brief comments about what went well and ideas for improving future events.

Make your travel plans well in advance, so you have room arrangements, transportation, and any other necessary plans in place before the tour begins. Be sure to plan for shipping or transporting promotional materials, copies of your book, and other necessary materials as well.

Managing a Successful Author Tour

Plan your travel time carefully to coincide with any interviews or other publicity events arranged in association with your author appearance. Get to the event location early, so you have plenty of time to set up tables, displays, equipment, or other items associated with your event. Give yourself time to handle the setup, with at least fifteen or twenty minutes to spare. Then relax and prepare yourself for your activity. Again, you want to appear calm, relaxed, and happy to be there, so your audience will be happy to be there, too.

After the event, be sure to assist with any necessary clean-up and thank the events manager or other individual you worked with in acquiring and organizing the event. Within a week of the event, send a follow-up note of thanks to the individual and ask for feedback on how you could have made the event more successful. If you feel there are possibilities for scheduling another event with the same person and locale, ask at that time, then indicate that you'll continue to follow up in the months to come.

Chapter 5

Conferences and Trade Shows

Trade shows, conferences, conventions, and other large-scale events offer opportunities to interact directly with a large number of potential book buyers. While this kind of event marketing could be a valuable marketing investment for you, you'll need to do your homework first. Will your booth bring you enough sales to make it cost effective? Can you expect to make many sales at a trade show? What is your *real* goal for attending a major event, and how can you best reach that goal? These are the questions you'll need to answer before you make the commitment to participate in a trade show, conference, or other large marketing event.

And, don't forget the many smaller events you can incorporate into your marketing plan. From starting your own book club to speaking to local businesses and offering demonstrations at retail outlets, you can boost public awareness and sales of your book through a broad variety of marketing events.

Choosing the Right Events for Your Market and Budget

No matter what your book's topic or genre, you can find a local, regional, or national conference, trade show, or other marketing event that will draw members of your target audience. If you are a fiction writer, there may be conferences and other events that are applicable to you, depending on your genre. For example, organizations like the Mystery Writers of America (*www.mysterywriters.org*) and Romance Writers of America (*www.rwanational.org*) may be able to point you to opportunities to market and sell your book.

As you pull together your marketing plan and budget, you're unlikely to have problems resulting from a lack of marketing opportunities. The larger issue will be determining *which* of the many possible types of marketing events available to you are right for your book's market and marketing budget. The following sections discuss some of the event types you might consider.

Book Trade Shows and Fairs

These large gatherings of authors and booksellers draw the attendance of professional book buyers, as well as members of the media, publishers, retailers, library representatives, and the general public. Most book trade shows and fairs run for two or three days. Vendors rent and staff booths to directly promote and sell books (some shows don't allow direct sales, however, so check the details before registering), as well as to make contacts for future sales.

Trade shows and fairs take place on the local, national, regional, and international levels, offering you the ability to "start small" before you commit to the expense of a larger event. Most of these shows charge booth space, "corner" space (open corners available in your booth), and many charge extra for tables, electricity, phone lines, and so on. Transportation, lodging, and meals, of course, would be added to these expenses.

Booth space at large trade shows and fairs can be quite expensive, as can nearby accommodations at the time of the event. Smaller regional events typically are less expensive and more cost-effective. These events typically offer a better opportunity to get face time with buyers interested in regional authors.

Again, if you decide that a book trade show is a good investment of your time and marketing dollars, look before you leap. Visit a few shows as an attendee, rather than an exhibitor, to get a feel for how they're organized, what kinds of books are being exhibited, and which types of exhibits seem most successful. And start small; you might be overwhelmed by a huge, national show, but a small local show might be very cost-effective, manageable, and an opportunity to determine whether you're interested in attending larger events.

> *Tradeshow Week* (*www.tradeshowweek.com*) offers a searchable online directory of trade shows. You can search specifically for book trade shows (choose "books" in the All Industry Categories drop-down box), then search for results by country, state/province, city, month, and year.

Conferences and Conventions

These events, like trade shows and fairs, typically draw attendees from a particular trade or industry, and offer vendors another opportunity for face-to-face contact with potential buyers. Some of these events are directed at a very specific niche market; if your book also occupies that "niche," attendance or speaking engagements can be especially beneficial for sales. If you can land a speaking engagement at a workshop or seminar associated with the event, you can gain even greater promotional benefits.

Conferences and conventions come in all sizes, of course, as do the costs associated with attending. And as stated earlier, you have a much more targeted attendee list at smaller events, and thus a better opportunity to reach *your* target market. Opportunities for arranging presentations and seminars at smaller events are also greater.

Book Festivals

These events typically offer vendors the opportunity for direct sales at retail prices. As when attending trade fairs and shows, you buy booth space and "work" the booth yourself, so you have invaluable opportunities for direct contact with large numbers of buyers who have come to the fair specifically for the opportunity to purchase books. You aren't dealing with as many professional buyers at these events, however, so booth space can be less costly, depending upon the size and popularity of the festival.

Again, look for small local festivals initially, then plan on moving to larger events after you've gained experience in managing a booth, handling direct sales, and promotional contacts with festival attendees. Most book festivals also have author readings and demonstrations, and so offer other promotional activities beyond sales at a booth or table.

Doing Your Research

You need to do some careful research and evaluation to determine whether *any* conference or trade show will be a worthwhile marketing investment. Beyond researching individual events to determine whether they will offer an appropriate environment for promoting and selling your book, you also must determine your specific goals for attending the event. Then you must analyze the associated costs and benefits of your attendance.

Most event Web sites list the event's important details. In addition to basic dates and locations, review the event agenda, the list of sponsors, exhibitors, and attendees. The online registration forms typically outline booth sizes and costs, floor plans, added expenses, and other important information for registrants.

With this information in mind, consider your goals for attending the event. Are you most interested in exposure? Or are you really interested in direct sales opportunities? Are you hoping to make contacts with professionals in a specific market or industry, with the possibility of expanding your contact list for future marketing efforts? Or, do you want a closer look at how a variety of authors and publishers are promoting other books within your topic area or genre? If the latter, can you benefit from simply attending the event, rather than participating as an exhibitor?

Most event Web sites also explain how to apply for making a presentation to event attendees. If you're interested in presenting at a trade show or conference, be sure to contact the organizers several months in advance, before the agenda and presenters have been finalized.

List your goals and then review them in light of what your research has told you about the event. Do the size, cost, attendee and exhibitor lists seem to describe an event that will help you reach all or most of your goals? Estimate your expenses and determine how those compare to the potential—and likely—benefits of attendance. This kind of cost/benefit analysis is important before you undertake any major marketing effort, but the potential expenses associated with trade show attendance give it special emphasis.

Attending Conferences and Trade Shows

If you determine that the benefits of attending outweigh the investments in time, effort, and expense, you can usually sign up online to attend an event. Follow the registration rules and deadlines carefully; frequently, rates go up as the event date approaches. Large national and international shows begin registering exhibitors a year or more in advance. Also, read the registration form and contract *carefully* before you agree to it. Most registration forms also list a contact person or office; use that contact to answer questions not covered on the Web site.

As with any event, you'll need to prepare in advance to be certain you have all promotional materials, media kits, handouts, and copies of your book available in advance of your departure. Be sure to take book order forms with you, in case you run out of available copies. If you'll be managing direct sales, take change and a lockbox for storing your money during the show.

The event manager will send you advance information for arrival, set-up, and tear-down. Most events also inform you of special rates in nearby accommodations. (If you're initially targeting local events, however, you can avoid this added expense.) If you can arrange for a friend to assist you in the booth, you'll have a better opportunity to interact with event attendees without watching your booth or missing other attendee questions. If you'll be working the booth alone, you might want to pack quick, easy-to-handle snacks and drinks, so you can grab a bite without deserting your booth.

Be prepared for some busy and potentially exhausting days in your booth. You'll want to be fresh, alert, and eager to talk to people visiting your booth, so plan to get plenty of rest. Networking at the event might turn into some great opportunities for after-hours meetings with other exhibitors or attendees, but be sure to return to your room in time to rest up for the next day's events. Be sure to take time to walk through the event, too; if you spend all of your time behind your booth table, you won't be able to learn from "the competition."

Finding Unique, Local Event Opportunities

Local chambers of commerce, convention centers, professional organizations, and so on are great sources of information about conferences and trade shows in your area. Internet searches on your topic area and the terms "trade show", "conference", and "festival" can also turn up valuable listings.

Don't limit yourself to traditional venues for promoting your book. Here are just a few ideas for creating promotional opportunities in your area:

~ Start a book club, or offer to make an appearance at an existing book club

~ Offer to teach a class on your book's topic area at a local community college, area arts center, or other community education facility

~ Contact local professional and social organizations to volunteer as a speaker

~ Offer to do a reading at your local library.

Remember, the more experience and contacts you can gain on a local level, the better prepared you'll be to expand your marketing to regional and national markets.

Chapter 6

Direct Marketing

If you send marketing materials to potential buyers through the mail, e-mail, or fax, you are participating in *direct marketing*. In Chapter 2, you read about techniques for sending periodic e-mail newsletters and other announcements to a select contact list of individuals and organizations. You've also learned about the anti-spamming laws that govern the distribution of marketing materials through e-mail and fax, and how creating an "opt-in" e-mail list can help you stay within the law when using this form of direct marketing. In this chapter, we focus on direct mail marketing, some effective techniques for using this form of direct marketing, and the rules you must follow to avoid becoming just another source of "junk mail."

Marketing through Direct Mail

If your mailing list is crafted to carefully represent members of your target audience, you can boost sales by marketing your book through direct mail. You can use direct mailings to announce special sales and promotions, to solicit book orders, to distribute brochures or newsletters, and to distribute news about upcoming book signings, workshops, speaking engagements, and other book-related events.

Direct mail marketing offers a number of benefits. You can mail to as few or as many recipients as you choose, giving you an opportunity to send out small mailings to test the effectiveness of your marketing materials. These limited mailings also enable you to distribute customized marketing materials to small, niche groups within your broader target audience. Direct mailings can be relatively simple and quick to produce, and you can get quick results as well. They're a very flexible form of marketing, too; in the same mailing, you can distribute a letter, brochure, and order form, or any other combination of marketing materials. And, you have an opportunity to interact with your target audience on a relatively personal level, as your mailings represent a form of "one-on-one" communication.

Creating Effective Marketing Tools

Because direct mail marketing takes so many forms, you have a wide range of possibilities for creating the materials you'll include in your mailings. But whether you're writing a sales letter or simply composing a card announcing an upcoming book signing, keep a few basic principles in mind:

~ Begin by determining specifically what you want to accomplish with the mailing. Are you building a contact list for marketing events? Are you recruiting attendees for a special appearance, reading, seminar, or workshop? Are you soliciting book orders? Know what you want to do, then craft your mailing and the recipient list to accomplish that purpose.

~ Be clear and direct. Speak directly to the reader, using simple, easy-to-read sentences.

~ State the benefit you're offering. If you are sending a sales letter, clearly and compellingly describe the benefits of reading your book. If you're offering a promotional copy, or discount on an upcoming workshop or seminar, or if you're distributing other news of interest to your targeted audience, say that clearly. Readers must be able to quickly understand specifically what they will gain from reading and (if appropriate) replying to your marketing mailing.

~ Tell the readers what they must do to gain that benefit—the call to action. Do you want them to fill out and return a survey card? Maybe you want them to place an order, sign up for an upcoming workshop, or show up at a book signing. Be sure to tie this response into the benefit you offer in the mailing.

~ Make the mailing easy to read and respond to. Your information should be compelling, but brief and well laid-out on the page, brochure, or mailer. If you are soliciting sales, be sure to include the phone number, Web address, or a pre-printed return mailer for the order.

As with many facets of your marketing campaign, start small in your direct mailings. "Test drive" a new marketing piece to a small segment of your target audience, to gauge its effectiveness. If your response is low, keep tweaking and testing the design. Alter the timing of your mailing, too, to help determine at what time of the month or year your mailings produce the best response.

You can design your direct mail pieces yourself, or hire a designer to do it for you. Some software programs, such as Microsoft® Office Publisher, enable you to add graphics, do a variety of page layouts, customize content, and use a number of other features to produce professional-quality direct mail marketing materials. If you need help writing and designing truly effective marketing materials, many small agencies, direct marketing companies, and independent freelance marketing consultants are available to help you with that effort. Look in the Yellow Pages for your area, or do an online search using the terms "direct mail marketing design."

If you're considering a direct mail campaign for your book, visit the Direct Marketing Association's Web site at *www.the-dma.org*. There, you'll find a valuable collection of useful information, including direct marketing techniques, industry tools, government regulations related to direct marketing, ethical "best practices" for direct marketers, upcoming seminars on direct marketing, and links to mailing services.

Gathering Your Mailing List

Creating lists from your own contact base is the best way to be sure that you're reaching your book's target audience. Your own contact list will typically be the best resource for your book's direct mail marketing program. But you also have the option of buying a mailing list. Many direct mail marketing services sell or "rent" mailing lists, based on regions, or targeted toward specific industries, organizations, associations, and other special interest groups.

Most of these sources will ask you to describe the group you want to target with your mailing; be very specific in describing your audience. Understanding your target audience is essential for any successful marketing campaign. And many direct mail pieces will be appropriate for only select members of that target audience, depending upon the objectives of each mailing. Mailing lists are available from a number of sources; an online search will produce a long list of such companies. The American Bookseller's Association will rent you a mailing list of bookstores. Visit the ABA Web site at *www.bookweb.org*. Open the site map and then scroll down to the Products and Services section to find information about their mailing list.

Handling Responses

If your mailing promotes a free review copy of your book, a promotional sweepstakes, or other offer, or if you use the mailing to solicit book orders, you must be prepared to promptly handle all replies. If you are targeting a relatively short list, this *fulfillment* step of your direct mail campaign should be manageable. Be certain, however, that when budgeting for a direct mail campaign, you've accounted for the cost of return mail, packaging, and so on. Also be aware that if you intend to fulfill book orders yourself, you'll need to have arranged for handling credit card orders, check, or other payment methods.

If you're targeting a larger mailing list, or if you don't want to handle the many issues of book order fulfillment, you should consider directing book orders to the AuthorHouse Bookstore. For other types of direct mail response, many direct mail companies offer fulfillment and reply services.

Check the offerings of any company you contract with, including their specific fulfillment services and costs.

Working with a Mailing Service

If you haven't the time or interest in sending out the mailing yourself, you can hire a direct mail firm to handle the distribution for you. Many direct mail companies also sell mailing lists. Mailing services can do more than just bundle and mail your marketing materials. Many services do all addressing, assemble multi-piece mailings, and search for the best postal rates for your marketing package. Most services also can be contracted to handle the replies to your mailing. Use the techniques described earlier in this chapter for locating a mailing service. Be sure that you understand exactly what services you're contracting for, and check rates carefully.

Understanding the Pros and Cons of Card Deck Marketing

Card deck (or *card pack*) marketing is actually a form of co-op marketing, in which a collection of cards, each carrying marketing information about a specific product or service, are bundled together and mailed as a group. This can be a cost-effective marketing technique, but only for certain types of books or promotions. Here are some advantages of marketing through a card pack or deck:

~ Card-deck mailings can be relatively inexpensive (typically averaging around $.02 - $.04 per contact)

~ Participating in these mailings is easy

~ Card decks offer a fast method of assembling new leads, and an equally quick assessment of how successfully you've defined the targeted audience for the mailing

At the same time, consider these disadvantages:

~ Several of your competitors might be included in the pack

~ You can't really target small niche audiences with such a mailing

~ You're limited in the quantity and type of information you can disseminate this way; you have the space of a single postcard to get your message across

Carefully consider the purpose of your mailing and whether it's well suited for this type of marketing. If you decide that card deck marketing may be for you, locate a card deck distributor by checking with a direct mail marketing company, such as Solar Communications (*www.solarcommunications.com*), or by conducting an online search using terms that include the topic area of your book and the words "card pack marketing."

Taking Care with Direct Mail

Although direct mail might be a great way to reach your target audience, you don't want recipients to view your efforts as just more junk mail. Here are some general guidelines:

~ Carefully control your mailing list; be sure you're mailing only to recipients that fall within your target audience.

~ Be up front about what the mailing offers. If you bill the mailing as a sweepstakes or giveaway, be certain to follow through with the promised return. If you're distributing a newsletter, be sure it actually contains news and information, rather than nonstop advertising and promotional text.

~ Honor recipients' requests to be removed from your mailing list.

The Direct Marketing Association maintains a "do not mail" list, and offers a guide to ethics and best practices for direct marketing (visit their site at *www.the-dma.org*, and look for the Ethical Best Practices Listing within the Government directory). For more information on the issue of junk mail, visit the Privacy Rights Clearinghouse (*www.privacyrights. org*). By carefully composing your mailing list, and by creating informative, useful mail marketing packages, you can avoid littering mailboxes with unwanted materials— and get the most benefit from any direct mail marketing program.

Chapter 7

Advertising

Advertising *must* work, or there wouldn't be so much of it surrounding us in our daily lives. But when you consider the broad range of advertising you see every day—from corporate names on auditoriums and stadiums to printed logos on coffee mugs and T-shirts—you begin to understand the number of decisions you'll need to make when determining whether and how to use advertising in your book's marketing plan. Your book, your audience, and your budget all play a role in determining how you can best, or whether you should, use advertising to help reach your marketing goals.

Advertising is cost-effective only when you take care to plan every phase of its design and placement. You'll need to research advertising types and venues thoroughly and strictly follow a pre-determined budget, which may need to include money for hiring an advertising agency or consultant. With this groundwork in place, you can determine the most effective ways to incorporate advertising into your overall marketing plan.

Targeting Your Advertising Dollars

Advertising is an area of book marketing that is rife with opportunities for overspending. To make the best investments in advertising, you must carefully target your expenditures. Which of your marketing goals are best met by advertising, and what kinds of advertising—print, in-store, radio, television—will best meet those goals? What kinds of advertising are most likely to reach the target audience for your book? And considering your total marketing budget and commitments, how much can you afford to spend on advertising?

Be a smart consumer when it comes to purchasing advertising. Rates for advertising vary, of course, depending upon the medium and the content of the advertisement. Look for ways to take advantage of discounted rates. Co-op advertising—in which you share advertising space with other advertisers—is a good way to save money. You also might be able to negotiate special rates based on running a series of ads over time, placing multiple ads in different locations within the same medium, buying leftover ad space (called remnant space), or allowing the ad to be accompanied by a short excerpt of your book. Finally, don't forget the use of promotional information placement to supplement advertising—in any medium.

Types of Advertising

When determining what type of advertising to use for your book, you need to consider how each medium can reach your target audience and how well it can showcase your book. You might choose to use a combination of advertising forms and formats, in order to reach different segments of your target audience, or to take advantage of specific opportunities related to marketing events, local attractions, organizational gatherings, and so on.

In any case, be sure to choose the advertising only after specifically identifying what you want the ad to accomplish and who you want it to reach. When you've determined the purpose and audience for your advertisement, be sure to choose the type of advertising most likely to meet both goals.

Advertising in Newspapers and Magazines

Newspaper advertising can be a cost-effective way to get the word out about your book. Rather than taking on expensive advertisement space in national newspapers, however, consider targeting local and special-interest newspapers that are likely to more directly appeal to your target audience. Which local, weekly, alternative, and special-interest newspapers do you read? Your own interests are likely to mirror those of your target audience, so that question gives you a good starting point for identifying good venues for your book's advertisement.

Next, consider where in the newspaper you might best place an ad to serve the purpose of your advertisement. Many papers carry a Book or Arts section, which might be a logical choice for advertising the release of your book or a special promotion to accompany an upcoming book signing. Are you using the ad to draw people to your appearance at a local festival, fair, or reading? If so, the "current events" section or a special advertising insert related to the event might be the best placement. If you're timing the ad to bring attention to a speaking appearance at a local organization or business, consider running a small ad in the business section.

Classified advertisements can be effective for reaching small niche audiences, such as car enthusiasts, bargain hunters, pet lovers, and so on. The classified sections of most alternative weeklies can be an especially effective way of addressing special interest groups.

If you've been able to negotiate a discount for multiple placements, you can also consider advertising in multiple sections of the same issue of the paper, or run the ad in different sections of the paper over time, to coordinate with your ongoing marketing opportunities and events.

> Coordinate your newspaper advertisements with other activities in your marketing plan. Remember to issue press releases to accompany appearances and to announce other newsworthy events associated with your book. Try to time your advertisements to coordinate with the publication of your press releases, to multiply the impact of both.

Magazines are even better vehicles for advertisements geared toward niche audiences. Magazines and trade journals by their very nature are designed to appeal to readers with specific interests. And many national magazines have regional editions, enabling you to speak directly to readers with local interests. Magazine advertising rates often are negotiable; when you contact the magazine's advertising department, ask for rates and any special discounts or promotional packages. The magazine also might be able to send you a media kit, with information about advertising submission deadlines, editorial contact information, and other advice for advertisers.

Advertising on Radio and Television

Television and radio advertising are less well-suited than print media for advertising books. That said, however, you might find ways to take advantage of local broadcasts over both media, depending upon your book's subject matter, target audience, and your specific goals.

You might, for example, run a short advertisement on drive-time segments of local radio broadcasts in the days preceding or following your appearance at a local event. If local current events have sparked an interest in your book's topic, you could take advantage of the moment by running short radio ads during news segments in which the event is likely to be discussed. And, if a local station airs a talk radio program in which your book's topic will be featured, advertising during that program could pull in some increased sales. Be sure to do your research; listen carefully to the program's broadcast during the times that you're considering advertising. Pay attention to the ads aired during those programs, to determine what listeners they target, and how they appeal to those listeners. Use that information to help you determine whether an advertisement for your book might be a good fit with the programming and audience.

A radio station will charge based on the length of your ad and the programming schedule. Advertising during prime times and popular programs might be an effective approach, but it will certainly be the most expensive. Seek the assistance of a professional radio merchandising company to help design your ads and determine the best placement for them.

You might also benefit from very specific types of advertisements on local television or public access broadcasts, but you must carefully weigh the costs against the potential benefits. Even local television stations can charge substantial advertisement rates, and the costs of preparing a television ad can be significant as well. Consider this venue only if you have significant funds to invest in advertising and if you have determined that television is the best way to achieve your specific advertising goals and target audience.

Public access broadcasts often run simple background or border advertisements surrounding announcements of local events. These types of advertisements can be inexpensive and effective, particularly if your book is of special interest to local readers. Most local access channels also provide some advice and assistance for preparation of their programming and advertisements. If you have watched the channel's programming and have determined that advertising there would meet your goals, contact the station's offices to request rates and to determine what kind of assistance the station can provide.

If you plan to go to the expense of advertising on local radio or television, it's particularly important that you coordinate the ads with other promotional efforts within your overall marketing plan. And remember that you also can promote your book on these media through a well-planned calendar of appearances, signings, and other marketing activities timed to coincide with area activities and local interests—with no advertising fees required!

Planning a Successful Advertising Campaign

Because we're surrounded by so much advertising, we've learned to filter out ads that don't quickly appeal to us by capturing our attention and speaking to a specific need. Effective ads must be well-designed, well-placed, and targeted to a specific purpose and audience. Every word and/or image used in an advertisement should be chosen to directly address those issues and goals. Although you can design simple newspaper advertisements, any substantial advertising campaign should be coordinated with an advertising professional.

Consider consulting with a local advertising agency or consultant; local consultants will have a better understanding of your regional marketplace, and can devote more time to your account than could a larger, national firm. Be clear about your goals when inquiring and find out about rates, previous work, and customer references. Then, compare proposed design with your own marketing goals as well as with other advertising for similar books before approving or paying for work.

Finally, remember that even if you're considering a broad national advertising campaign, you'll need to test your strategies first in smaller markets. If you're using multiple advertising formats and media, use codes or other methods for tracking response, so you know which ads do best. Learn from your advertising experiences; build upon the ideas that work, and abandon those that fail to produce results.

Chapter 8

Retail Sales

Almost every author wants to see his or her book on retail store shelves throughout the country. With the number of titles published every year, however, there is stiff competition for the available shelf space. Whether you are a publisher or an author, there are numerous hurdles to overcome in getting book retailers to stock any given title. By learning the fundamental processes of the book sales channel and retail bookselling, you may be able to manage a profitable retail sales program for your book.

Understanding the Book Channel

Every item sold in any marketplace comes to the final consumer through its own particular sales process or channel. Traditionally, a typical book retail sales channel has involved these basic processes:

~   A publishing house publishes the book

~   The publishing company's sales force presents the book to buyers at various booksellers

~   The booksellers sell the books to consumers

In the retail book channel, buyers at booksellers determine what books are available for consumers to buy by making decisions as to which books they will stock in their retail locations. Their decisions are based on their perceived potential for a given book. If they guess wrong, they always have the option of returning unsold copies after a given period of time. These are called *returns*. This mechanism limits what book products are created by publishers, as they need to focus their attention on books that retail buyers will buy.

The Internet and print-on-demand publishing, however, are changing the overall book selling model dramatically. With the level playing field of the Internet, the convenience of at-home and at-work shopping, and no need to print and warehouse copies of new titles, any book has a viable opportunity to reach its targeted audience. Book retailers have been slow to adapt to the opportunities afforded to them with self-published titles. While this makes it more difficult to get self-published titles onto bookstore shelves, it is not impossible if you understand how the system works. As an author, you can decide how important the retail segment is to the distribution of your book.

Getting Your Book to Market: Ingram and Lightning Source

When you publish your book through AuthorHouse, the books are printed by Lightning Source. This print-on-demand company is a subsidiary of Ingram, the world's largest wholesale book distributor. By using Lightning Source, your book is automatically listed and carried by Ingram. Having your book listed through Ingram is important; most book retailers in the United States can or do buy books from Ingram. Once a book is in Ingram's system, it is then available to over 25,000 booksellers for direct retail sales.

To be offered for sale through the Ingram distribution model, your book must have an ISBN identification number. (AuthorHouse acquires this number for you.) Buyers use this number when ordering copies of your book. With the print-on-demand publishing model, when Ingram receives orders for your book, the copies are printed by Lightning Source and shipped to the bookseller or end-consumer. Ingram offers these print-on-demand titles at a lower discount rate than that applied to books from traditional publishing houses. With no inventory and stocking charges, print-on-demand titles produce much higher profit margins for authors than most would receive from the royalty payments offered by traditional publishers.

After your book is "live" in the AuthorHouse system, it may take as much as thirty to forty-five days for the book to become available through retail channels. Time your promotional efforts accordingly, so that your book will be available immediately when customers attempt to buy it.

Getting Your Book into Brick-and-Mortar Bookstores

Selling books to national brick-and-mortar bookstores such as Borders or Barnes & Noble can be a difficult task. Buyers for these chains can be inaccessible to individual authors. That doesn't mean you need to abandon your dream of seeing your book displayed on a bookstore shelf, however; you can make it happen, with some planning and concentrated effort.

Rather than trying to "break down the wall" to get national distribution through a large bookstore chain, your best bet is to start small and build your entryway one brick at a time. Many bookstores have an interest in carrying titles by local or regional authors. Begin your own retail efforts for this part of the book sales channel by visiting bookstores in your area. Try to arrange a book signing or reading event, either at the bookstore or at a local library, adult learning center, or other venue. If you can build local interest in your book, you're more likely to enjoy good local sales. When your book sells well through local outlets, it can gain wider placement throughout the national level.

Don't concentrate all of your efforts on the chain bookstores, however. Independent bookstores frequently are more willing than "the big guys" to give new authors a platform for promoting their books. Most have a loyal local following with a real interest in the work of local authors. Again, work with the stores to organize a promotion plan for your title, by arranging a signing, a book reading, a special sales promotion, or other event that can build business for you and the store.

If you are trying to get your book stocked with a book retailer, you must understand the concept of returns. To hold down their own storage and inventory costs, booksellers stock limited copies of individual titles that haven't yet "proven themselves" in the marketplace. To avoid being saddled with unsold copies, booksellers buy from sources that provide a *returns* policy. If bookstores know that they can return and receive credit for unsold books, they can confidently order multiple copies of books in anticipation of their sale. A return program encourages bookstores to order your book and makes it easier to arrange book signings, since the store can stock up on extra titles, without fearing that they'll be left holding unsold inventory.

Selling through Web-based Outlets

Most self-published authors sell the majority of their books through online outlets such as Amazon.com, BarnesandNoble.com, and AuthorHouse.com. These outlets are important to self-published authors, because they provide a simple sales model that provides a level playing field in the "shelf presence" of a book. In essence, the Internet has become the storefront of choice for self-published authors. When a customer orders a book online, the book can be printed individually and shipped directly to the customer.

When you publish your book through AuthorHouse, your book is automatically included in the company's online bookstore, AuthorHouse.com and sent to Amazon.com and BarnesandNoble.com. Customers can order your book directly from any of these sites, and AuthorHouse handles all of the details of fulfillment, from collecting the payment and processing your author royalty, to printing and shipping the book to the customer. Although other online sites have their own submission and sales policies, most handle all sales, collection, and fulfillment responsibilities, enabling you to benefit from the sale, while avoiding the mechanics of taking and filling the order.

Once your book has an ISBN and is "live" in the Ingram system, the book is immediately available at the AuthorHouse Web site at *www.authorhouse.com*. It customarily takes about twenty-one days for a book to appear as available for sale at Amazon.com and BarnesandNoble.com. To find information for listing your book with any other online bookselling site, go to the bookseller's homepage and click on a link to Publisher and Author Resources/Guidelines, or search on those terms using the site's search engine.

Working with Bookseller Programs

Each site offers its own programs and features that enable you to tell potential buyers more about your book and promote its unique value in the marketplace. You should view every online bookseller listing as both a sales *and* promotion opportunity.

Each online bookseller offers its own selling programs. Amazon.com, for example, offers its Advantage program, which provides twenty-four-hour shipment on most books, access to Amazon marketing programs, and easily tracked accounts information, in addition to other features. Amazon's Paid Placement program also enables you to pair your book with another title at a reduced rate to the buyer, potentially boosting sales and providing more visibility for your book.

You can learn more about listing your book with Amazon. com and its programs at *www.amazon.com/publishers.*

The online sales outlets offer readers numerous advantages as well. For example, Amazon's "Search Inside™" program enables shoppers to read your book's cover copy, table of contents, and a sample chapter or excerpt. To maximize your book sales through Amazon, you can participate in these programs.

Soliciting Reader Reviews

Most online outlets also offer reviews and ratings, from both professional reviewers and the book's readers. These reviews offer you another great way to improve your book's sales. Have family, friends, and associates write and post reviews of your book, to help discuss its strong points and to generate more interest in the book from would-be book buyers who are browsing the online bookseller's site. The reviews needn't be "over the top" in their praise to make a difference in your book sales. The more solid, positive reviews you have, the more likely would-be buyers are to take notice of your title and, perhaps, go on to buy it.

Finally, both Amazon.com and BarnesandNoble.com enable readers to create and post lists of their favorite books. You can help publicize and promote your book by creating a list of your own; include your book's title along with those of similar books. When anyone searches for the titles of any book on your list, the entire list—including your book—will appear as a search result. This simple step gives your book added publicity and can lead to improved online sales.

If your book receives positive reviews in print, online, or on a radio or television broadcast, be certain to send that review to the online booksellers with which you sell your book. Most will allow these reviews to be posted on your book's information page. Check with each site's submission policy for details.

Selling through Other Outlets

Retail sales opportunities don't end at the bookstore's doors (or online portal)! With a little creativity and a lot of well-directed market research, you can find numerous locations that offer unique and valuable opportunities for selling your book directly to the public.

Thinking Outside the Bookstore

As an author, you may love to read and, as a result, you might be a regular visitor to your local bookstore. On the other hand, lots of people rarely—if ever—go into a bookstore, even though they occasionally buy books. As you conduct your daily business, take a moment to notice how many places offer books for sale. You are likely to discover that many of those places aren't even retail outlets. From health clubs to professional organizations to convenience stores, wherever people with common needs or interests conduct business or gather for recreation, you can find a potential outlet for selling your book.

When considering where you might try to place a few copies of your book for sale, think about your book's unique content and the audience to which it "speaks." Your market research has already helped you determine who your target audience is and what unique need or interest your book fills for that audience. Take that information to think of locations where your book could reach your potential readers.

Here are just some of the many types of locations that might provide great retail opportunities for your book:

- ~ Antique shops
- ~ Art supply stores
- ~ Banks
- ~ Book clubs
- ~ Craft and hobby shops
- ~ Community centers
- ~ Convenience stores
- ~ Electronics stores
- ~ Farmer's markets and food stalls
- ~ Gift shops
- ~ Golf pro shops
- ~ Hardware stores and home improvement centers
- ~ Health clubs
- ~ Historical associations
- ~ Homeowner's organizations
- ~ Insurance agencies
- ~ Libraries

~ Museums

~ Niche retailers (gourmet food shops, hiking outfitters, decorating centers, card shops, etc.)

~ Pet shops

~ Religious centers and organizations

~ Restaurants

~ Social/service clubs

~ Schools

~ Salons and spas

~ Supermarkets

~ Veterans' organizations

~ Wine retailers

~ Youth centers

This list represents only a fraction of the possibilities available to you in your community and region—and through your interests and those of your book's target audience. Be imaginative; you have nothing to lose and much to gain from placing your book in as many locations as possible.

Managing Retail Sales

Whenever you place your book for sale in any location, you'll need to work with the location's management or staff to gain their approval for displaying and selling your book, and to determine a plan for handling the actual book sales. Ideally, the location's personnel will be willing to handle and record all business transactions for some percentage of the sale price.

Be prepared to clearly and compellingly explain to the location's manager or buyer why your book will appeal to its customers, clients, or members. Also, be willing to work with them on an appropriate discount and sales commission. Have a plan for managing and restocking your display, and then be sure to follow up frequently, to check on book sales and to restock as necessary.

As with many areas of your book's marketing program, you can learn from experience in retailing your book. Note the locations where your book sells strongly, and try to determine what factors are contributing to those sales. If you discover that your book does better than you expected with a specific location or niche audience, are there other ways you can target that location or group? Use the information you gain from your retail successes to boost sales at less productive locations and to identify new ones.

Chapter 9

Guerrilla Marketing

Marketing your book doesn't require you to become a high-powered salesperson, advertising executive, or seasoned promoter. Your personal involvement and commitment to the process are the most important factors for a successful book marketing campaign. Your creativity, imagination, and energy will also contribute to the success of your marketing efforts. Use the low-cost and unexpected ideas outlined below as a launching point for crafting your own "guerrilla marketing" campaign.

Becoming a "Guerrilla Marketer"

The term "guerrilla marketing" is used to describe a broad variety of non-traditional, low-cost, and effective techniques for promoting a product or service. Authors are among the champions of this marketing movement; with a keen understanding and commitment to their product, authors are uniquely suited to devise new, interesting, and successful techniques for reaching their book's target audience.

After you've spent time identifying and profiling your book's target audience, and reviewing the successful marketing techniques used to promote other books in its genre, you'll be well-prepared to come up with your own unique marketing ideas. Here are some guerrilla marketing ideas you can use for inspiration as you brainstorm:

~ **Insert marketing materials in your correspondence** such as your invoices and your own bill payments.

~ **Offer promotional items as door prizes or giveaways** at your author appearances; examples include T-shirts, calendars, baseball caps, or coffee mugs, printed with the name and cover of your book, and the address of your Web site or online sales portal.

~ **Place an ad with your local movie theater**, to appear during the slide show that plays before each movie begins.

~ **Run specials on your books**, such as buy one, get one free or referral discounts.

~ **Hold raffles or contests** at local fairs and events, where the prizes are free copies of your book or promotional items.

~ **Became a sponsor** for community events, such as theatrical performances, fund drives, farmer's markets, youth-related events, and state/county fairs. Run an ad in the printed program or other material that accompanies each event. Be sure to attend the event, and work the crowd, distributing bookmarks or other promotional materials. If possible, set up a booth for book sales and "meet the author" opportunities.

~ **Print small chapbook excerpts** from your book (perhaps a ten-page preview) and distribute them to members of the media and potential buyers. Alternatively, you can create electronic versions of the chapbook and distribute them via e-mail. In either case, be sure that the last page of the chapbook tells readers how to order your book.

~ **Publish an e-newsletter** pertaining to your book's main themes, for example cooking, gardening, genealogy, or local history; advertise your book within the newsletter.

~ **Make handbills** and hand them out to passersby in shopping areas or during lunchtime or after-work hours near business centers.

~ **Offer to speak** before local organizations. Contact the area chamber of commerce to find out about the organizations in your region, then send the organizations information that describes you and your book and what you might offer as a speaker.

~ **Host a monthly reading group** to get in front of book buyers. Although you shouldn't feature your book as the "book of the month," you will have drawn together a group of attentive readers who you can tell about your book (and who are likely to tell others).

~ **Host a writers' workshop** and schedule weekly, bi-weekly, or monthly workshop events where local writers get together and critique each other's work. These meetings offer great word-of-mouth publicity, as well as an opportunity to network with other writers in your community.

~ **Do a regional book tour** to promote your work. Extensive book tours are costly, but you needn't plan a globe-hopping, international blowout. If you can schedule appearances or events in a few key markets—such as in major cities or regional centers—you can really boost public awareness of your book.

~ **Host your own events** such as "whodunit" mystery dinner theaters, poetry readings, square dances, or parties linked to any day or event that ties into the topic of your book (consider special days such as Halloween, Columbus Day, Boxing Day, St. Patrick's Day, or even Take Your Daughter to Work Day).

Consider setting up a calendar that will target your guerrilla marketing activities to specific dates and events throughout the year.

Be Innovative, but Plan Wisely

Once you begin brainstorming, you might be surprised at how many creative and non-traditional methods and opportunities you can come up with for marketing your book. Guerrilla marketers need to plan carefully, however, to be sure that their promotional techniques will be effective and well-received.

Plan your marketing activities well, to be certain that you are able to carry them off without disappointing or annoying participants, business owners, event organizers, and so on. Here are just a few of the ways you can be sure that your marketing efforts will be effective:

~ Have promotional items ready for distribution, and put together a working plan for holding giveaways or raffling off items.

~ Check with retailers or business owners before you distribute marketing materials within their space.

~   Don't put posters or other notices in the windows
of restaurants, retailers, or other businesses without
first getting the permission of the owner.

~   Target your speeches or other appearances to offer
real value to the groups you're addressing.

You can be proud of your book, and you should draw upon
your creativity when determining effective ways to market
it. Just be certain that your marketing tactics are carefully
planned, organized, and carried off, so that you get the full
benefit of the time, effort, and money that you invest in
them.

Appendix A: Glossary

Advertising: the public promotion of a product, business, or service.

Anti-spamming laws: federal, state, or local regulations prohibiting the distribution of sales/promotional information through e-mail, fax, the mail, or other mass-distribution medium.

Banner ads: graphic boxes used to advertise on Web sites; banner ads can contain animation, review quotes, cover art, and—always—a "click here" link to take readers to another Web site or online sales portal.

Banner ad network/exchange: a cooperative advertising group in which members exchange and post banner ads on their Web sites.

Blog: (also *Web log*) an online journal or news site regularly updated to reflect the author's interests, ideas, and pursuits.

Book channel: the processes and services involved in taking a book from the publishing house to the end consumer.

Book signing: an event in which an author signs copies of his or her books for individual buyers, usually after a short reading and/or question-and-answer session.

Brick-and-mortar: a term used to describe physical sales, business, and manufacturing facilities, as opposed to online sites or shopping portals.

Card deck (card pack): a marketing technique in which a series of cards carrying advertising and ordering information about individual products and services are bundled and sent together to potential buyers.

Chat room: an online forum for exchanging messages and information on shared interests with other chat room members.

Click-through rate: charges assessed for Web advertisements based on the number of visitors who click to access the advertiser's Web site.

Contact list: a list of people, businesses, organizations, and media and their accompanying addresses, phone numbers, other information useful when making contact with that individual or organization.

Co-op marketing: a marketing arrangement in which multiple sellers combine advertising and promotion messages into a single marketing piece to share the costs of production and distribution.

Demographics: recognizable characteristics of a group of consumers, including age, gender, income, education, locations, interests, and so on.

Direct marketing: sending marketing materials directly to potential buyers, typically through the mail, e-mail, or fax.

Distribution: marketing and supplying goods to retailers and consumers.

Domain name: the name of an individual or business that is included in a Web address, usually appearing between the protocol identification (http://www.) and suffix (.com, .net, .gov, .org, and so on).

E-commerce: online selling, typically involving the acceptance of credit card information, the establishment of site security, and an order fulfillment process.

E-mail blasts: mass-mailings of information sent through e-mail.

E-mail opt-in list: subscription lists through which individual subscribers give their permission to be contacted through e-mail with news, sales, and promotional information; in a *confirmed* opt-in list, the service source replies with an e-mail verifying the subscriber's intent to join the service.

E-zine: electronic publication, typically distributed online or via e-mail.

Ingram: the world's largest wholesale distributor of books.

ISBN: *International Standard Book Number,* a unique and internationally recognized identification number assigned to a book.

Fulfillment: the process of receiving orders for, packing, and shipping books.

Guerrilla marketing: using non-traditional methods to advertise and promote your product.

Link: A Web address or *URL* that, when clicked, takes online users directly to the addressed Web site.

Lightning Source: a subsidiary of Ingram and print-on-demand company.

Livejournal: a site devoted to the creation and ongoing maintenance of online "communities" devoted to a number of topics and areas of interest.

Marketing: advertising, promoting, and selling a product or service to retailers and/or end consumers.

Market research: the gathering and analysis of information regarding consumer groups and competitor businesses in order to determine the preferences and buying habits of the consumers and to define the successes and failures of competitors within that market.

Media directory: a directory of various media outlets, their practices, and their contact information.

Media kit: a collection of material, including news, marketing materials, and background information, which can be sent to representatives of the media to help publicize a product.

Niche markets: narrow and closely defined areas of a target audience that share a particular need, idea, or interest related to a specific product or service; *niche retailers* are those whose products or services cater to a niche market.

Online retailers: businesses that sell products through online (Internet) shopping sites (also referred to as *Web-based outlets*).

Pay-per-click advertising: a form of advertising (also known as *search marketing*) where advertisers bid for specific keywords to be associated with their product or service. When a user visits the search engine and enters search terms including the keywords, a link to the advertiser's Web site or shopping portal is returned as a prominently displayed result for the search. Advertisers are charged each time a searcher clicks on the link in the search results list.

Podcasting: a communication method that involves creating and distributing a broadcast—a news update, announcement, or even a short "radio" program—to a list of broadcast subscribers. Messages are recorded using special RDF XML technology. The resulting file can be "read" by any digital audio player or computer with audio-playing software.

Pop-ups: advertisements that appear when a user accesses a Web site.

Press release/news release: short (typically, one-page) announcements of newsworthy events associated with a person, business, or product.

Print-on-demand: a technology used to rapidly print individual books as they are ordered, in quantities as few as one, rather than producing and warehousing copies in anticipation of later sales.

Promotion: disseminating information about a product or service to potential consumers and retailers, with the purpose of encouraging them to purchase the product or subscribe to the service.

Publicist: someone who helps promote a business or product.

Public relations (PR): managing and increasing public awareness about a product, business, or service.

Reciprocal links: links exchanged and posted by two or more Web sites.

Review copy: a free copy of a book sent to a journalist or reviewer, in the hope that the recipient will write and publish a review of the book.

Restocking: renewing an inventory of products after sales have depleted the original stock.

Returns policy: a program that enables retailers to return for a refund unsold copies of a book after an agreed-upon period of time.

Sales portals: online sites that sell directly, using secured ordering information, payment methods, and other aspects of ecommerce.

Search engine: a Web-based utility used to search for and compile a list of related sites on the Internet (sites with a shared topic, purpose, or content).

Spamming: bulk distributions of advertising information, typically through e-mail or fax.

Target audience: a group of people identified as those most likely to be interested in a particular product.

Trade show: large gatherings of buyers, vendors, media, and others interested in products or areas of interest. Vendors rent and staff booths to directly promote and sell products, as well as to make contacts for future sales.

URL (uniform resource locator): a URL identifies the location of Web pages on the Internet.

Web log: see *Blog*

Web hosting service: a service that makes a Web page available to visitors online.

Web site: a collection of information, images, and other content accessed online through a single address.

Appendix B: AuthorHouse Resources

AuthorHouse offers a number of promotional products and services you can choose to purchase and use when marketing your book. As part of our ongoing efforts to support authors, we do continually evaluate the range of support services we offer. As a result, new services may be available that are not described here, and the specific details of these services may change as needed. For complete details on current options and pricing, or to purchase any of the services described below, contact your AuthorHouse representative at 888.519.5121.

Press Release Distribution Services

AuthorHouse provides a number of public relations-oriented services. You can choose the service that's right for you, depending on your interest and budget.

~ With the *Standard Promotion* option, an AuthorHouse professional will compose a press release about your book and distribute it to 100 media outlets, targeted to your book's topic and selected geographic locations. We will also provide complimentary review copies to the media upon request.

~ The *Expanded Promotion* option provides all of the features of the *Standard Promotion*, but increases the number of media outlets to 500. This option also includes the *Book Signing Kit* (described below) to support your public appearances.

~ The *Personal Media Valet* program gives you the benefits of ongoing public relations support. The *Personal Media Valet* requires the purchase of the *Expanded Promotion*, and provides follow-up contacts after the press release distribution to pursue potential articles, interviews, or book reviews. The package also provides contact with select bookstores to inquire about potential book signings and appearances, and customized stationery for corresponding with the media and other contacts. The service lasts for thirty days and includes a weekly report of results.

~ If you want assistance with making ongoing media contacts after your book has been announced, the *Media Alerts* package provides up to five separate press releases to announce book signings, appearances, awards, or any newsworthy event associated with your book.

~ The *Newswire Plus* package forwards your professionally written press release to a number of databases, Internet sites, Web portals, and online brokerage firms in the United States.

Advertising Services

If advertising is an important part of your marketing campaign, you'll find that advertising in major national venues can be expensive. AuthorHouse offers two co-op advertising packages that can get your book listed in important national publications at special reduced rates:

~ Through a special arrangement with *The Bloomsbury Review*, we make it possible for authors to advertise in a publication respected by libraries, booksellers, and bookstores around the nation. AuthorHouse will place your full-color advertisement and ordering information as part of a full-page ad featuring twelve AuthorHouse books. *The Bloomsbury Review* reaches over 125,000 readers in the United States and Canada.

~ If you've never before been published, you can join eleven other AuthorHouse authors in placing an advertisement in the Sunday edition of *The New York Times Book Review*. This publication reaches over 1.7 million readers.

Marketing and Promotions Kits

To make the most of author appearances, book signings, conferences, and other events, you may need some promotional materials you can hand out to attendees and passersby. With these materials on hand, you're always ready to promote your book, no matter what the occasion or setting. AuthorHouse has two programs of useful collections of materials for promoting your books:

~ The *Marketing Kit* includes bookmarks, business cards, and postcards containing your promotional text, professionally designed and illustrated. If you'd prefer to stock up on just the materials of most interest to you, you can also purchase any of these individual items in bulk.

~ The *Book Signing Kit* provides everything you need to set up and promote a successful event. The kit includes posters, flyers, invitations, a list of bookstores, and a handy instructional booklet that helps you prepare for the event.

Don't forget to ask your author services representative about volume book discounts. If you want to stock up on copies for sales at appearances, book signings, festivals, and other events, you can receive a sizable discount for buying in bulk.

Bookseller's Return Program

Booksellers are more willing to stock up on multiple copies of a book when they know they can return any unsold inventory. If you purchase the *Bookseller's Return Program,* your book is listed through Ingram as being returnable, making it more appealing to retailers. In addition, you receive a kit which includes customized postcards that announce your book's returnable status for distribution to bookstores and other retailers, a list of bookstores in the largest city near you, and more expert advice on selling to bookstores. The program lasts for one year.

Registration Services

AuthorHouse also offers a number of services that can help you take care of the "nuts and bolts" functions associated with publicizing and marketing your book:

~ **Obtaining a Library of Congress (LOC) Control Number.** Libraries across the nation use LOC numbers to identify and catalog books. AuthorHouse can assist you in obtaining this number, making your book much more accessible to libraries. AuthorHouse also sends a copy of your book to the Library of Congress, where it will be permanently stored in their archives.

~ **Copyright registration.** AuthorHouse also can register a copyright for your book, in your name, with the U.S. Copyright Office.

~ **Web domain registration.** AuthorHouse can purchase and register a customized Web address (URL) for you, using the address name of your choice (pending availability, of course).